EAT FAT, LOSE W

Also by Ann Louise Gittleman, M.S.:

Beyond Pritikin
The 40/30/30 Phenomenon
Before the Change
Get the Salt Out
Get the Sugar Out
Your Body Knows Best
Super Nutrition for Women
Super Nutrition for Men
Super Nutrition for Menopause
Guess What Came to Dinner
Beyond Probiotics
How to Stay Young and Healthy in a Toxic World

EAT FAT, LOSE WEIGHT

How the Right Fats Can Make You Thin for Life

Ann Louise Gittleman, M.S.

with

Dina R. Nunziato, C.S.W.

KEATS PUBLISHING

LOS ANGELES

NTC/Contemporary Publishing Group

Eat Fat, Lose Weight is not intended as medical advice.
Its intent is solely informational and educational. Please consult a
health professional should the need for one be indicated.

Library of Congress Cataloging-in-Publication Data
Gittleman, Ann Louise.
    Eat fat, lose weight: the right fats can make you thin/
by Ann Louise Gittleman with Dina Nunziato.
    p.   cm.
Includes bibliographical references and index.
ISBN 0-87983-966-X
    1. Reducing diets.   2. Essential fatty acids in human nutrition.
I. Nunziato, Dina. II.   Title.
RM222.2.G537 1999
613.2'5–dc21
                                                    98-49592
                                                        CIP

Published by Keats Publishing,
a division of NTC/Contemporary Publishing Group, Inc.,
4255 West Touhy Avenue,
Lincolnwood, Illinois 60646-1975 U.S.A.

Design by Robert S. Tinnon

Printed and bound in the United States of America
International Standard Book Number: 0-87983-966-X
10 9 8 7 6 5 4 3

To Americans everywhere
who are striving for optimum health
and effortless weight loss

Contents

Acknowledgments

I AM SINCERELY GRATEFUL to the many clients and professionals who have been so supportive of my work over the years. First and foremost, thanks to my editor Phyllis Herman whose professional expertise coupled with keen editing skills makes her an author's dream. Also, I wish to acknowledge the wonderful assistance provided to me by Dina Nunziato who helped me in transforming my ideas into a full-fledged book. And, of course, much appreciation is extended to Stuart Gittleman who provided me with research assistance throughout the project.

Many thanks to all of the essential fatty acid pioneers who have paved the way, including Dr. Hazel Parcells, Dr. Royal Lee, Dr. Bernard Jensen, Dr. Johanna Budwig, Udo Erasmus, Dr. David Horrobin, Dr. Artemis Simopoulos, Dr. Donald Rudin, Clara Felix, and Dr. Robert Erdmann. Kudos to the oil manufacturers in the natural foods industry like Barleans, Spectrum Naturals, Flora, Arrowhead Mills, and Health from the Sun whose products reflect the highest standards of purity, uniformity, and taste.

Finally, my most heartfelt appreciation to my readers and associates who have supported my "eat fat, lose weight" message. I am indebted to the radio hosts and hostesses across the land who have also supported this message with true missionary zeal, especially Joanie Greggains, Mark Stowe, Joan Hamburg, Deborah Ray, Don Bodenbach, and National Public Radio.

Introduction

J UST AS I WAS SITTING DOWN to write this introduction, my
mother sent me an interesting packet of news clippings.
My mother, you must understand, is one of my best research
assistants. She scours the newspapers and magazines of my
native New England looking for articles relevant to my work.
The first article in the packet was a lead story in the May 27,
1998 *Hartford Courant* entitled "Revising the Reputation of
Fat." The article explained that, contrary to popular belief, not
all fats are bad and that certain fats actually contain nutrients
that are absolutely essential for human development.

My mother's attached note said, "Ann Louise, you have been
saying this for years!"

She's right. Ten years ago, my now prophetic book *Beyond
Pritikin* was released. *Beyond Pritikin* was the first book of its
kind to promote a revolutionary new eating plan, one that
added certain fats to the diet. Radically different from the
widely acclaimed no-fat, high–complex-carbohydrate diet that
Nathan Pritikin had pioneered (which became all the rage in
the 1980s and early 1990s), *Beyond Pritikin* attempted to educate
the American public about the importance of the good fats.
And I knew what I was talking about. I was the first nutritionist

in the country to observe the long-term effects of going fat free. I had been Director of Nutrition at the renowned Pritikin Longevity Center in Santa Monica, California, from December 1980 to 1982. Later, in my own practice, I witnessed firsthand the increasing health problems of fat phobia.

The message in my first book, *Beyond Pritikin*, was simple: While not all fats are good (especially those that are hydrogenated, fried, or heat processed), not all fats are bad either; some are even essential. The problem was not that most Americans were eating too much fat, but that they were eating the wrong kinds of fat.

As a matter of fact, I proposed that a diet rich in the healthy fats (like olive oil) and the essential fatty acids of the omega-3 family (found in fish oils and flaxseeds) and the omega-6 family (evening primrose oil) was absolutely vital to the total health of the body from head to toe. I knew back then that fatty acids work in the system by transforming into tissuelike hormones called prostaglandins, and that these prostaglandins are responsible for the healthy regulation of the reproductive, immune, cardiovascular, and central nervous systems.

Some of my colleagues thought I was crazy. Hadn't I seen the impressive results of the latest low-fat/high-carbohydrate diet plan? How could I risk my professional reputation by going against an overwhelming cultural and marketing phenomenon?

I knew what I was up against. Countless individuals questioned me about my findings. I couldn't appear on a talk show or radio program without fielding the same questions over and over again: Wasn't it true that eating fat just makes you fatter? Didn't I know that fat contained nine calories per gram, while protein and carbohydrates contained only four calories per gram? How could consuming fat help you lose weight? Hadn't it been proven in Third World countries that a low-fat, high-carbohydrate diet was the key to weight control? How dare I promote an increase in fat consumption?

Eat fat *and* lose weight! This was absolute heresy in the decade of fat phobia.

Yet, I was compelled to educate the public about the truth. In banishing all fats, I believed we had thrown the baby out with the bathwater. All fats are not created equal. In fact, certain fats boost the body's metabolic rate and protect the heart and nerves. As easy as it was to believe that you could only put on pounds by eating fat (and boy, was it easy), *it simply wasn't true!* In fact, a lot of what was being said about the dangers of all fat in general was untrue. More than one diet guru in the fat-free decades spouted so-called facts about fat that weren't supported by a shred of scientific evidence. I believed then, as I do now, that weight gain may be more related to the nation's overconsumption of fat-free carbohydrates (which stimulate insulin production and, therefore, fat storage) than a result of the healthy consumption of essential fats.

Well, thankfully the time has finally come to set the record straight. After a twenty-year love affair with low-fat dieting, many people have begun to realize something disturbing. They feel *worse* than they did before they jumped on the fat-free bandwagon. Far from recognizing their goals of weight loss and increased vitality, most Americans have gained weight and lost energy. Many feel constantly fatigued and tire easily. Some are plagued with symptoms of food allergies, bloating, mood swings, and uncontrollable sugar cravings. Many are beginning to question the simplistic, flawed data about fats and oils that continue to predominate in our national nutritional guidelines.

Being "ahead of the curve," as I was with *Beyond Pritikin*, sometimes had its frustrations. Yet, it is now tremendously gratifying to see the media finally popularizing ideas I pioneered ten years ago. When I see articles on "Good Fat/Bad Fat" and books promoting "40/30/30" (carbohydrate/protein/fat) ratios, I am thrilled—thrilled to have been at the forefront of a revolution whose time has finally come.

In this book, I explain why the low-fat/high-carbohydrate craze of the last two decades has failed. I reveal why the no-fat and reduced-fat foodstuffs that have taken over supermarket shelves actually work to promote bingeing and fat storage. And, most important, I demonstrate why certain fats are not only permissible, but are also essential—essential to the health and vitality of every human being, regardless of age, gender, or current weight.

I begin by exploring the misinformation and deceptions that permeate the fat-free diet craze. You'll learn the truth behind the "big fat lies" and find out why Americans really get fat on all those no-fat diets. I explain the inherent dangers in a high-carbohydrate diet, including the connection between carbohydrate overload, insulin resistance, and fat accumulation. We'll look at the myths surrounding cholesterol, heart disease, and fats and focus on the importance of sustaining adequate protein levels for lean muscle mass and increased metabolic rates.

Further on, I will fill you in on some little-known facts about the omega fats. You'll learn about the satiety nutrient that enables you to feel full and satisfied after a meal and how you can boost your fat-burning potential by actually increasing your intake of certain fats and oils.

Because of their often overlooked importance in a balanced nutritional plan, I assigned specific chapters to each of the omega-3, omega-6, and omega-9 families of oils. Included in each chapter is important research information about each of the different omega oils, their benefits, special uses, and how to combine them for optimal health and weight management. I also devote a specific chapter to omega remedies for overall health, focusing not only on weight loss but also on current health issues such as healing depression, recovering from allergies, and improving immune system disorders with the omega oils.

For your convenience, whether you eat out or prepare your own meals, I have created the most easy-to-follow breakfast, lunch, and dinner plans. These are weeklong menus that include a shopping substitution list to help you as you begin to incorporate my eat fat, lose weight plan into your healthier lifestyle.

While the title of the book is *Eat Fat, Lose Weight*, this book is not solely about weight loss. It is a book about understanding the body's basic nutritional needs and responding to them. For those of you who are carrying excess weight, following my nutritional plan will undoubtedly help you reach your goal. But if I were to provide you only with information on losing weight, I would be doing you a disservice.

This is a book about health, about achieving and maintaining a healthy weight, as well as healthy percentages of body fat, lean muscle tissue, and strong bones. It is about living well and being well throughout your lifetime.

EAT FAT, LOSE WEIGHT

CHAPTER ONE

The Big Fat Lie

T HE AMERICAN PUBLIC HAS BEEN BRAINWASHED with a great big fat lie—a lie that has been told, retold, and told again over the past fifteen years. It is a lie that, in my opinion, has resulted in widespread harm to the overall health of our nation.

This lie, one of the biggest marketing hoaxes of the twentieth century, is that fats are the ultimate dietary killers. What's more, the lie has been extended to cover all fats, not just a few harmful ones. Many of the nation's food companies would have us believe that all fats are harmful, despite widely known scientific evidence that fats are, biochemically speaking, very different from one another. Just pick up any newspaper or women's magazine and you can learn all of the newest, most creative ways to slash the fat, cut the fat, lose the fat, or lower the fat. We've been told that we can eat whatever we want, whenever we want, all the time, as long as the food we are eating is fat free. Unfortunately, doctors, dietitians, and others who should know better seem to have forgotten that fat happens to be an essential nutrient, necessary for the health and well-being of our bodies and our brains.

Advertisers have learned that the words *fat free, low fat,* or *reduced fat* translate into an instant sales boost. Just take a look at how low-fat Snackwells have replaced Oreos as the nation's best-selling cookie. The magic adjectives "low fat" and "fat free" seem to convey to us that we have unlimited permission to scarf down whole boxes of the stuff—without getting fat! (More on this in chapter 2.)

So let's look at the evidence. Since we as a nation have gone fat free, here's what has happened:

1. Obesity has increased more than 23 percent.
2. Adult-onset diabetes has skyrocketed.
3. The incidence of certain kinds of heart diseases has increased.
4. Depression has become a widespread national disorder.
5. Immune system viral infections like chronic fatigue and other illnesses are rampant.

While every disease is not necessarily associated with a fat-free diet, the fact is that these diseases have increased while fat intake has declined. This is a phenomenon that begs to be investigated. While it is true that Dr. Dean Ornish's low-fat diet (along with lifestyle factors like meditation, yoga, and stress reduction) has reversed heart disease in some cases, the dangerous message we keep getting is that *all* fat is *all* bad *all* the time.

IT'S THE TYPE OF FAT THAT COUNTS

Although Americans are too fat, I believe in reality many are suffering from an essential fatty-acid deficiency. That's right. Many of us are starved for certain kinds of fats. This deficiency may be contributing to the rise in breast cancer, attention deficit disorder (hyperactivity), depression, diabetes, arthritis, immune system dysfunction, and PMS and menopausal problems, not to mention nail, hair, and skin problems like eczema and psoriasis. As a nutritionist for the past two decades, I have discovered that the majority of my female (and increasingly male) clients suffer from a condition known as "fear of fats." They have been programmed to believe that fat is bad and must be eliminated from foods, via fat-free cooking methods, the intake of no-fat foods, and the conscientious counting of fat grams. Instead of healthy fats, my clients have loaded up on sugars and carbohydrates like rice cakes, breads, pastas, and potatoes. Sadly, by eliminating all fats (even the healthy and essential ones) from their diets, many women actually gain weight, feel depressed, and suffer from PMS and perimenopausal symptoms like mood swings, irritability, water retention, and breast tenderness.

I first discovered the value of healthy fats in the early 1980s when my female clients absolutely raved about the virtues of an essential fat called gamma linolenic acid (GLA.) Found primarily in evening primrose and borage flowers, GLA works wonders in treating allergies, eczema, arthritis, and premenstrual syndrome. My patients happily reported that when they began taking GLA, the mood swings and cramping they experienced during their menstrual cycle disappeared. As I have continued my extensive research in this area, much of which I will share with you in this book, I have discovered that essential fats like GLA, along with many others, are absolutely vital for everyone at every stage of both the male and female life cycles.

WHY SOME FATS ARE ESSENTIAL

Essential fatty acids are necessary because the body cannot produce them on its own. There is no such thing as an essential carbohydrate or an essential sugar, but there is essential fat. It's what our nutritional textbooks years ago called vitamin F. You need to take it in from a food source or food supplement. Quite the opposite of the fat phobia that is out there today, it is absolutely critical that we begin to understand the importance of taking in these essential fats.

So where and how do we come by these essential fatty acids? They're primarily derived from two families of fatty acids called the omega-3s and the omega-6s. The highest amounts of omega-3 oils of one particular variety are found in fatty fish like salmon, anchovies, sardines, and mackerel. There is also a vegetarian source of omega-3 fat, high in an essential fatty acid called alpha linolenic acid, that can be found in flaxseeds, the vegetable purslane, and to a lesser degree walnuts, soybeans, and pumpkin seeds. The highest amount of omega-6 oils can be found in nuts, seeds, and botanicals like evening primrose oil and borage oil. (I will say more about these oils in chapters 8, 9, and 10.)

Essential fatty acids are necessary for the production of the group of hormonelike chemicals called *prostaglandins*. Prostaglandins are essential for the entire body's cellular functioning—from the tiniest cells to the largest of the vital organs. Healthy prostaglandin functioning is critical in the body's fight against a wide variety of conditions ranging from arthritis and ulcers to migraines and cancer. They also boost the functioning of the cardiovascular, reproductive, immune, and central nervous systems.

Essential fatty acids can dramatically contribute to health and vitality throughout life—beginning with the development of the infant brain. Over half of the brain is composed of fat. Brain chemicals called *neurotransmitters* are regulated by the prostaglandins that are created by the essential fatty acids. There is a particular kind of omega-3 essential fatty acid known as docosahexaenoic acid, or DHA, which is absolutely essential for brain and eye development. (I will discuss DHA in detail in chapter 8.) Prevalent in fatty fish and plant algae, this omega-3 fatty acid is the major fat present not only in the brain but also in the retina of the eye. DHA is also well known for its ability to promote learning functions and to stimulate the brain's auditory and visual perceptions. Both the omega-3 and omega-6 essential fatty acids are components of the outer membrane of every cell in the body where they protect against viruses, bacteria, and allergens. The brain—and indeed the entire central nervous system—needs fats for nourishment and protection.

There is frightening evidence to suggest that the previous three generations of Americans have not been eating the right kinds of fatty acids for the development of the brain. Could this be a reason we have so many children diagnosed with attention deficit hyperactivity disorder (ADHD)? America's children are being diagnosed right and left with ADHD and are being prescribed the drug Ritalin. These kids are not suffering from a Ritalin deficiency. There are studies to suggest that these children are suffering from essential fatty acid (EFA) deficiency because some of the clinical signs of EFA deficiency are restlessness, short attention span, irritability, mood swings, and even panic attacks. When children diagnosed with ADHD start eating the right kinds of fats, many parents notice that their children become calmer and more focused.

Mother Nature did a brilliant job of combining the omega-3 and omega-6 oils in the most immune-protective food ever created—mother's milk. Cow's milk, on the other hand, has little. For this reason, I firmly believe that omega-3 supplementation should be recommended for every pregnant woman. Moreover, it should also be added to baby formula due to its crucial role in brain development and immune protection.

Wait a minute. I can hear you worrying—if I include more fat in my diet, I'm just going to get fatter! Contrary to what most of us have been taught to believe (that eating fat will make you fat), dietary supplementation with an essential fatty acid has actually demonstrated significant reduction in body weight and fat by stimulating the oxidation of fat. Scientists and nutritionists now believe that the building blocks of the essential fatty acids increase metabolic rate and positively affect the body's ability to burn fat. Eating fat to promote fat burning? That's right. My female patients who supplement their diets with foods or food supplements high in certain kinds of fat report surprising weight-loss results. These women do not diet, per se, but take the special fat nutrient GLA to control their PMS problems, recurring yeast infections, and arthritis. Many of my clients are amazed that they can eat fat and lose weight at the same time. The difference, of course, is that they eat the right kind of fat. The right kind of essential fat will actually stimulate the mechanism in the body that burns fat. This internal fat burner is what scientists call brown fat. (More about this in chapter 7.)

Plain and simple, our bodies couldn't function without fats! Perhaps this is why the American Heart Association suggests that we should consume up to 30 percent of our total calories from fat. Fats are required for the production of hormones; they facilitate oxygen transportation and calcium absorption; and they assist in the absorption of the fat-soluble vitamins A, D, E, and K. Healthy fats nourish the skin, nerves, and mucous membranes, and by providing essential fatty acids they undoubtedly benefit the immune, cardiovascular, reproductive, and central nervous systems. There really is no other nutrient on earth that can heal the body from head to toe and keep it healthy from infancy to old age like the essential fats.

The big fat lie is that all fat is harmful. The actual truth is that not all fats are created equal. Indeed, they are quite different. There are healing fats and there are harmful fats. Unfortunately, we have been exposed to misguided and distorted nutritional information that has grouped all fats, from healthy olive and flaxseed oils to the dangerous transfats in margarine, shortening, and fried foods into the same undesirable category.

Rather than blaming *all* fats for our ills, we need to look more carefully at the types of fats we have been eating and, consequently, attempting to avoid.

In November 1997, researchers in Boston published the results of their extensive Nurses' Health Study in the *New England Journal of Medicine*. The study, in which 80,000 nurses between the ages of thirty-four and fifty-nine were followed for fourteen years, reported that contrary to popular belief, "it's not the *amount of fat* you eat, it's the *kind of fat*." "The best solution is to decrease saturated fats and avoid transfats," said the lead author, Dr. Frank Hu of the Harvard School of Public Health. "And replace these unhealthy fats with healthy ones—monounsaturates and polyunsaturates from natural vegetable oils."

A basic rule is that the body is accustomed to fats that occur in foods naturally. Some naturally occurring fats are more beneficial than others, but, in general, the body can process natural fats much more easily than fats altered by man-made processes. Natural fats, especially unsaturated natural fats like the omega oils, are particularly suited for efficient use. Pliable and soft, unsaturated natural fats are easily formed into the necessary elements for the body's needs. As I noted earlier, these natural fats are components of all the vital organs, including the brain and nervous system.

THE FATS TO AVOID

At the other end of the health spectrum from the natural fats are the transfats. Transfats are rigid and difficult for the body to process. I'll talk a lot more about them in chapter 4, but for now, let me explain that in transfats the fat molecules have been chemically transformed so that the body cannot identify them as natural fats. If the body doesn't recognize them, chances are it's not going to know how to process them efficiently or effectively. Research has shown that transfatty acids contribute to impaired cellular function, clogged arteries, and degenerative disease. We also know they are believed to interfere with the body's ability to efficiently process good fats.

Both fried foods and margarine, for example, contain fats that are harmful. The fats in fried foods have been transformed by high temperatures into transfats. Most of us know that fried foods aren't good for us, but what's wrong with margarine? Simply put, margarine is not the natural form that vegetable oil takes. Margarine is a "hydrogenated" food product, which means that its oils have been artificially processed to make them stiff and more easily used in food preparation. Unfortunately, hydrogenated fats contain the harmful transfatty acids associated with accelerated aging and degenerative diseases like heart disease and cancer.

How, you may be wondering, am I supposed to figure out which fats to eat, which fats to avoid, and how much "good fat" is too much? Throughout this book, I will help you negotiate the often confusing maze of information on different types of fats, the quantities you need to stay healthy, and which fats to eat throughout your lifetime to promote efficient fat burning and lasting weight loss.

CHAPTER TWO

Why Americans Get Fat on No- to Low-fat Diets

B Y NOW WE ARE ALL AWARE that Americans are eating less fat today, and yet, as a nation, we are fatter than ever before. The U.S. Department of Agriculture has reported a 14-pound drop in red meat consumption between 1980 and 1990. In the past twenty years, butter intake has dropped by a whopping 25 percent, but, at the same time, the per capita ingestion of sugar has increased by 20 pounds per person, per year. That's an astonishing amount of sugar we're consuming! The number of overweight people in America has ballooned, not necessarily because of increased fat intake but because Americans are drastically overeating sugar and carbohydrates, which quickly add up to increased calories and increased fat storage.

FAT-FREE CALORIES ADD UP

When manufacturers create their low- and no-fat products, they almost always add sugar, and sometimes salt, to maintain some semblance of taste. For example, three regular Entenmann's chocolate chip cookies contain 11 grams of sugar. If you try to be "healthier" by going for three of their low-fat cookies, you'll end up with 12 grams of sugar! But, you say to yourself, I've surely saved on calories. Not necessarily so. By opting for the low-fat serving, you have saved yourself a mere 20 calories (140 versus 120) and paid for your caloric savings with added sugar, a danger we will explore in detail in chapter 3.

Most clinicians who work with overweight individuals agree that, in an attempt to steer clear of fat, many dieters reach for foods laden with sugar and simple carbohydrates, ironically the very carbohydrates that can stimulate fat storage. Dieters often incorrectly assume that "nonfat" means "nonfattening." Conversely, they also believe that dietary fat always ends up as body fat, a myth that I debunk in chapter 6. Rather than opting for healthy proteins, vegetables, and fruits, dieters in search of fat-free foods often stock up on low-fat muffins, bagels, cereals, rice cakes, and other high-glycemic carbohydrates (see chapter 3), which trigger the fat enzyme lipoprotein lipase to store excess calories as fat and raise insulin levels.

Too many of us have been led to believe that if something is labeled "low fat" we can eat all we want and not gain an ounce. As enticing as that is to believe, it is simply not true. In fact, my experience shows that people who choose low-fat foods will actually consume quantities far in excess of what they would have normally eaten had the food not been touted as low fat. How many times have you reached for extra cookies because they were advertised as low in fat? Would you have been so quick to eat as many if they were full of fat?

Recently, nutritionist Barbara Rolls and others conducted a study at Pennsylvania State University to research the role that caloric information plays in total calorie consumption. These nutritionists gave yogurt snacks to fifty women. The first study group was instructed that the snacks were low in fat. The second group was cautioned that they were high in fat. And the third study group was given the snacks with no information as to calorie content. Later in the day, the researchers discovered that the group who believed they had eaten a low-fat snack ate more calories at their subsequent meals. As ironic as it may sound, believing you are eating a low-fat food may actually encourage overeating!

FAT AND SATIETY

While the phenomenon illustrated by the yogurt snacks appears to be purely psychological (believing a food to be low in fat gives you license to eat more of it and more of everything else), I also believe there is a physiological element to why eating low-fat foods seems to promote eating greater quantities. First, you must understand that fat is the *satiety nutrient*. Compared to all other nutrients, it does the best job of helping you feel satisfied and full after eating. I've seen time and again how people following low- or no-fat diets eat seemingly large quantities of food, only to be left feeling hungry and unsatisfied a short time later. Unlike sugar and carbohydrates, the satiety nutrient is digested slowly in the body and gives a sense of satisfaction after a meal. After eating a relatively small quantity of the satiety nutrient, the brain registers a feeling of satisfaction and fullness. Small amounts of foods containing healthy fats (like peanuts, almonds, and pumpkin seeds) can go a long way toward promoting good health and creating a sense of satisfaction. The satiety nutrient also functions to lubricate the intestines, encouraging healthy, regular bowel functioning.

Because low-fat diets leave people feeling unsatisfied, they tend to eat more and more frequently than on a diet with a moderate, healthy fat content. And, unfortunately, I have been witness many times to accounts of dieters who try to "be good" all day, only to be left starving and craving fat by evening. Is it any wonder that so many dieters binge on cookies and ice cream at night? It's not a lack of willpower, it's the body craving the fat it needs to survive. What's important is to consume fat intelligently. And I don't have to tell you that it is next to impossible to be intelligent about the choice of fat when you're starving, cranky, and tired. You must eat moderate amounts of the right fats strategically throughout the day to maintain a sense of fullness and satisfaction and to prevent the over-whelming sense of hunger that occurs on a low-fat diet.

THE DIFFERENCE BETWEEN LOW-FAT AND LOW-CALORIE FOODS

The confusion between low-fat and low-calorie foods was exacerbated by the recently fashionable idea that fat calories were more powerful and more harmful than those derived from protein or carbohydrates. Early in the low-fat craze, sci-entists believed that dietary fat was converted to body fat quicker and more easily than were carbohydrates or protein. Many researchers now acknowledge that this process is much less notable than early reports indicate. Dr. Rudolph Leibel, an obesity researcher at Rockefeller University in Manhattan, notes that "metabolically, the difference between conversion of fat or any other food is so minute as to be largely irrelevant to dieters. A calorie is a calorie." Dr. Leibel goes on to say that "research has found that after a while on little to no fat, the body begins to compensate for the absence of fat in the diet by becoming more efficient in converting other food sources into body fat." This means that after months or years of low- to no-fat dieting, the body actually becomes *better at creating fat*!

Most obesity researchers have found that there is no relationship between fat intake per se and flabby thighs. "A moment on the lips" does not automatically mean "forever on the hips"! Dr. Walter Willett, chairperson of the Department of Nutrition at the Harvard School of Public Health, notes that "the percentage of fat in a diet probably has nothing, or very little, to do with weight loss or maintaining weight loss. A number of long-term randomized trials have looked at this. It appears that calories are what really count, and not the percentage of calories from fat."

As far as weight gain is concerned, it's the total calories ingested that matters, not the calories from fat. The last decade provides the proof: Even as we cut back on fat, our weight has increased steadily—an average of eight pounds per person. We may be eating less fat, but we are consuming more and more calories; a trend driven in part by the assumption that we can eat all the low-fat food we want and not gain weight.

Americans have been conditioned to believe that more is always better—and this is especially true when it comes to food. If we can find a way to "get away with it" calorically, we will eat and drink until we are stuffed. "Getting away with it" is why the fat-free craze is so incredibly appealing. But at what cost?

In February 1998, Procter & Gamble Co. introduced their

Frito-Lay's Ruffles and Doritos chips made with olestra. Olestra, a synthetic fat substitute concocted from sugar and vegetable oil, is being marketed as the ultimate in fat-free products. With molecules too large to be absorbed into the digestive tract, olestra is passed through the system and eliminated before it can add calories. The only problem is that olestra causes serious digestive side effects, from diarrhea to abdominal cramping and loose stools. The marketing strategy behind olestra will undoubtedly play on Americans' fear of fat and the desire to "get away with it."

Dr. Dean Ornish, the author of *Eat More, Weigh Less*, notes that "the week Entenmann's rolled out its fat-free desserts, a number of our patients gained weight. They thought that as long as they were eating something fat free, they could eat as much as they wanted."

Eating as much as you want and getting away with it—a disturbing notion to some and a dream come true for others. I often wonder why it's so important for people to cram their bodies full of food—way past the point of fullness. I believe this occurs, in large part, because the foods we are reaching for, mainly sugars and refined carbohydrates, are not satisfying or nutritious. I also believe we have drifted far from the idea of reasonable portion sizes and comfortable fullness.

SIZE DOES MATTER

Think for a moment, if you will, about the idea of a reasonable serving size in this day and age. On the one hand, we have food labeling—what you find listed in tiny print on the side of nearly every item you purchase in the supermarket. This labeling tells us a "serving" of cereal is a ¾ cup or a "serving" of cola is ½ can. While I don't advocate drinking soda, I don't know anyone who routinely stops at half a can! On the other hand, we have the marketing geniuses at fast-food restaurants who routinely tell us how much happier our lives will be if we just "supersize it." Enlarging our combo meals for just pennies, we can have gargantuan quantities of fries and soda with our double cheeseburgers.

We are approaching a real crisis with respect to portion sizes. Mammoth muffins, oversized bagels, and mounds of "fat-free" pasta encourage us to ignore portion control. The gigantic restaurant-size portions simply don't match up with the USDA recommendations. A restaurant serving of pasta (3 cups), for example, is nearly six times as much as the USDA-suggested ½ cup serving.

The gross discrepancy between USDA portions and "marketing" portions is leaving consumers confused and at a loss to determine appropriate quantities for consumption. In my own experience, I frequently see clients who don't know why they are not losing weight even though their food intake and exercise levels appear admirable. They will routinely report eating "normal" helpings during their meals. When we look closely, however, I frequently find that their "normal" portions are in fact double or triple the calorie intake they thought they were consuming. This underestimating of calorie intake appears to be epidemic, even among savvy, nutritionally educated Americans.

Like the Americans who consume them, food portions have been growing larger and larger each decade. This growth has been so steady and insidious that it often escapes our notice.

For example, in the 1930s a bottle of Coca-Cola was 6½ ounces. Now a super-sized soft drink at McDonald's is 32 ounces— nearly five times larger!

TRADING FAT FOR CARBOHYDRATES

Recommendations about low-fat diets have only caused people to eat more sugar and more calories, says Frank Sacks, a researcher at the Harvard School of Public Health. "For our society there is good evidence that a moderate-fat diet would be healthier than a low-fat diet." We hunger for fat-laden foods because our bodies and our brains need fat. All fats provide energy, maintain cell membranes and blood vessels, transmit nerve impulses, and produce essential hormones. However, as we have already noted, some fats are more valuable than others in promoting health and well-being.

I am very concerned about the carbohydrate-related health problems about which so many of my clients who have traded fat calories for carbohydrate calories are complaining. Carbohydrate overloading often occurs at the expense of protein- and antioxidant-rich foods that are necessary for immunity, steady blood sugar levels, proper hormonal functioning, and tissue repair. Moreover, the popular, high-glycemic carbohydrates that everyone is eating—bread, pasta, and potatoes—are deficient in the essential fatty acids that control the cardiovascular, reproductive, and nervous systems. To make matters worse, as stated earlier, these high-glycemic carbohydrates actually encourage fat storage by triggering the lipoprotein lipase enzyme and elevating the fat-promoting hormone, insulin.

As a result of a decade-long binge on carbohydrates, many Americans are suffering from food cravings; lack of mental concentration and energy; aging skin, hair, and nails; fluid retention; high triglycerides; weight problems; and the need for more and more sleep. The time has come to stop the carbohydrate craze.

CHAPTER THREE

The Carbohydrate Myth

AMERICA'S OVEREMPHASIS on carbohydrates is backfiring. The promotion of carbohydrates at the expense of proteins and essential fats has left many teetering on the edge of metabolic chaos. I have counseled countless women and men who have actually gained weight following the trendy high-carbohydrate regimen. They eat large quantities of pastas (hold the oil!), breads, and potatoes (hold the butter or sour cream!), precious little animal protein, and virtually no fat whatsoever. They fill up on all the "fat frees" out there today—yogurt, salads with no-fat dressings, low-fat cookies, fat-free potato chips, and gallons upon gallons of aspartame-laden soft drinks. Are they thin? Hardly. In fact, they're more likely to be tired, edgy, bloated, and suffering from a whole host of mental and physical ailments, from yeast infections to depression. But, miraculously, when they cut back on carbohydrates and reintroduce lean proteins and essential fats into their diets, their symptoms disappear and their weight drops.

Not only can you gain weight on a diet containing too much of the wrong kind of fats, you can also become overweight on a diet too high in carbohydrates. A number of the most popular diet plans out there today are unusually high in carbohydrates and therefore deficient in protein and the essential fatty acids—which we are now discovering are the true keys to overall good health.

There are two types of carbohydrates: simple and complex. Simple carbohydrates are the sugars, mainly table sugar and natural sweeteners, the fructose in fruit and the lactose in milk. Complex carbohydrates are found in starches, legumes, and vegetables. What you may not know is that carbohydrates can be rated on a "glycemic index," which measures the rate at which they are converted into blood sugar.

THE GLYCEMIC INDEX

The glycemic index* is a listing of foods that shows the rate at which a carbohydrate breaks down into sugar or glucose in the bloodstream. Foods with a high glycemic index are considered to be fast acting because they release glucose into the bloodstream quickly, causing a rapid rise in blood sugar, which in turn signals the pancreas to produce insulin, the hormone that removes excess sugar from the bloodstream and signals the body to store fat. Foods with a low glycemic index are considered slow acting and release glucose into the bloodstream slowly, providing the brain and body with a longer-lasting, steady energy level for several hours.

Becoming familiar with the glycemic index makes it possible to decide which foods to eat plentifully, moderately, or

*Adapted from my book *The 40/30/30 Phenomenon.*

sparingly. The foods with a high glycemic index are the most rapid inducers of insulin; these are the ones to avoid. Sometimes it is possible to offset one high-index food with several low-index foods; balance is the key. Even more important, knowledge of the glycemic index of carbohydrates makes it possible to avoid the effects of unknowingly eating several high-index foods together.

The following points are worth keeping in mind as you look over the glycemic index on pages 24–25:

- Although refined carbohydrates are sometimes listed in the same category as whole-grain products, they are much less beneficial because they lack the vitamins, minerals, and fiber that whole-grain foods possess.
- When proteins and fats are eaten with high- or moderate-glycemic foods, they help slow down absorption of the carbohydrates and therefore help prevent sharp rises in blood sugar and insulin levels. Thus, a baked potato eaten with a piece of chicken, a small pat of butter, or olive or flaxseed oil is fine.
- Energy levels are closely tied to the foods you select. The higher the food on the glycemic index, the faster the burst of energy and the sooner the letdown. Foods lower on the glycemic index provide a healthier, more long-term kind of energy.

If you would like a brand-name list of acceptable and unacceptable foods based on the glycemic index, contact the Glycemic Research Institute, 601 Pennsylvania Avenue, Suite 900, Washington, D.C. 20004.

THE GLYCEMIC INDEX OF CARBOHYDRATES

RAPID INDUCERS OF INSULIN

Greater than 100 percent
Puffed rice
Corn flakes
Maltose
Puffed wheat
French baguette
Instant white rice
40-percent bran flakes
Rice Krispies
Weetabix
Tofu ice cream substitute
Millet
Most refined cereals

100 percent	*90–99 percent*
Glucose	Grape Nuts
White bread	Carrots
Whole-wheat bread	Parsnips
	Barley
	Muesli
	Shredded wheat
	Apricots
	Corn chips

80–89 percent	*70–79 percent*
Oatmeal	Corn
Oat bran	Rye flour
Honey	Shortbread
White rice	Ripe banana
Brown rice	Ripe mango
White potato	Ripe papaya
	All-Bran
	Kidney beans
	Wheat (coarse)
	Buckwheat
	Oatmeal cookies

MODERATE INDUCERS OF INSULIN

60–69 percent
Raisins
Mars candy bar
Spaghetti, white
Spaghetti, whole wheat
Pinto beans
Macaroni
Bulgur
Couscous
Wheat kernels
Beets
Apple juice
Applesauce
Pumpernickel bread

50–59 percent
Potato chips
Barley
Green banana
Lactose
Peas
Sucrose
Yam
Custard
Dried white beans
Lima beans
Rye (whole grain)

40–49 percent
Sweet potato
Navy beans
Split peas
Bran
Peas
Oats, steel cut
Butter beans
Grapes
Oranges
Orange juice

LOW INDUCERS OF INSULIN

30–39 percent
Apples
Pears
Tomato soup
Ice cream
Black-eyed peas
Chickpeas
Milk, skim
Milk, whole
Yogurt
Fish sticks, breaded

20–29 percent
Lentils
Fructose
Plums
Peaches
Grapefruit
Cherries

10–19 percent
Soybeans
Peanuts

THE INSULIN CONNECTION

As you have undoubtedly experienced, eating too many highly processed, high-glycemic carbohydrates can quickly trap you in a rapid sugar-craving cycle. The more high-glycemic carbohydrates you eat, the more insulin is produced. As the insulin takes the excess sugar out of your bloodstream, your energy level drops and your brain sends out the message to increase the blood sugar by eating more carbohydrates. You find yourself bingeing on carbohydrates as your blood sugar zips up and down. Fatigue follows every downswing, and soon you're trapped in the nightmarish cycle of high-glycemic mania. Think about the last time this happened to you. Do you remember what triggered the sugar cycle? Many women I have counseled report this cycle occurring on an almost daily basis, beginning with a breakfast of no-fat, sugar-free (but aspartame-laden) yogurt and continuing throughout the day with sugary snacks, coffee, and diet drinks, and finally ending at night with an entire box of low-fat cookies.

Dr. Stephen Gullo, the director of the Institute for Health and Weight Sciences in Manhattan, notes that many of his patients in recent years continue to gain weight even on a low-fat diet. This appears to be the result of replacing dietary fat with simple, highly processed carbohydrates like low-fat cookies and rice cakes rather than with the slower-acting, low-glycemic carbohydrates found in many vegetables and fruits.

Most of the carbohydrates that my clients consume are high glycemic—either the simple carbohydrates found in sugars and sweeteners or the highly refined carbohydrates found in refined cereals, muffins, bagels, pastas, pastries, and the like. These high-glycemic carbohydrates are transformed very quickly by the body into glucose. From there the glucose can be sent to one of two places: If we are exercising regularly, glucose can be used immediately by the muscles for energy production; if not, it will be stored for future use. When we overeat high-glycemic carbohydrates, we are left with an abundance of glucose, more than the body could ever need or utilize immediately. The glucose that is not used right away by the muscles through exercise is stored in the liver and muscles as glycogen. But the body is only able to store a small percentage of excess glucose as glycogen. The rest is converted and stored as—you guessed it—fat!

High levels of fat-free, refined carbohydrates work to sabotage the best dieting efforts in another way as well. High levels of insulin, triggered by high-glycemic diets, may block the critical pancreatic hormone glucagon from operating effectively within the body. Glucagon's primary function is to unlock stored body fat, enabling the body to burn that storage fat for energy. If there is too much insulin in the body, glucagon is essentially blocked from unlocking the fat, and the body is denied its ability to use the fat banks it has been saving. Excess carbohydrate consumption locks the doors to stores of fat! The result is more and more fat accumulating in the body, none of it ever being made available for conversion to muscle energy.

HOW THE RIGHT FAT CAN HELP

I firmly believe that the only way to emerge from the carbohydrate craze with our metabolisms intact is to reintroduce moderate amounts of healthy fats into the American diet. Again, like a knight on a white horse, healthy fats can rescue us from our carbohydrate mania. Healthy fats, in addition to exercise, level out blood sugar. As a slow-burning nutrient, fat actually slows down the release of carbohydrates into the system and improves the ratio of insulin to glucagon, essential for mobilizing stored body fat. Remember, if you have too much insulin in your system, your glucagon is essentially blocked from unlocking all the fat you have been storing away. Well, guess what? Healthy fats are the key to unlocking the fat banks your body has been saving so that you can begin burning stored fat as muscle energy. Unlike highly processed, high-glycemic carbohydrates that can create food cravings, healthy fats will unlock stored fat reserves, help keep the appetite satisfied for up to six hours at a time, and protect against the temptations of sugary snacks.

Simple sugars and highly refined carbohydrates must be selected carefully and not overconsumed. I advocate the elimination of all refined carbohydrates and recommend additional proteins, fats, and the complex carbohydrates (found in low-glycemic vegetables and fruits) to take the place of problematic high-glycemic carbohydrates. See chapter 12 for menu plans that balance carbohydrates with adequate amounts of protein and health-enhancing essential fats.

The U.S. Department of Agriculture's Food Guide Pyramid, which received so much positive media attention because of its departure from the four-food-group approach to good nutrition, also promotes the carbohydrate craze. Drastically underemphasizing the need for fats and oils containing essential fatty acids, the Food Guide Pyramid recommends six to eleven daily servings of bread, rice, and cereals. Unfortunately, the pyramid makes no distinction between healthy whole foods (whole-grain breads and brown rice) and highly refined, ultra-processed carbohydrates. Manufacturers of all types of highly processed breads and cereals delight in their ability to lay claim to their place at the broad base of the Food Guide Pyramid, and Americans continue to consume tremendous quantities of highly refined carbohydrates every day.

INSULIN RESISTANCE

The vast quantities of carbohydrates many Americans consume and do not burn due to sedentary lifestyles has taken its toll. We see the results in the skyrocketing numbers of Americans afflicted with adult-onset diabetes and its precursor, insulin resistance. Researchers estimate that as many as 75 percent of the American population may have tendencies toward insulin resistance, a condition created by an imbalance in the amount of insulin that controls the body's blood sugar. Insulin-resistant individuals can develop glucose intolerance, high insulin levels, high triglycerides, low HDL cholesterol (the "good" cholesterol), hypertension, and Type 2 diabetes. Those who are insulin resistant respond to carbohydrates by overproducing glucose, which leads to an overproduction of insulin and the stimulation of fat storage. Dr. Richard Heller, who with his wife, Dr. Rachael Heller, authored *The Carbohydrate Addict's Diet*, maintains that "the majority of overweight people are insulin resistant. Carbohydrates are the worst thing they can eat because it causes them to overproduce insulin, which stimulates appetite, encourages the production of body fat and, over the long term, has serious health implications."

Insulin resistance developed eons ago when our ancestors had to cope routinely with periods of feast interrupted by long periods of famine. During times of abundance, the body overproduced insulin. This overproduction enabled the liver to convert glucose into fat to be stored and used in times of deprivation. If the body had not been able to overproduce insulin and thereby secure fat storage, the glucose would have been used immediately for muscle tissue and organ functioning. Insulin resistance enabled our ancestors to store the fat they needed to survive long stretches without adequate food sources. Fortunately, most of us no longer live in an age of caloric deprivation. Our supermarkets are stockpiled with foodstuffs to feed large armies several times over. Unfortunately, however, many have not yet made the complete adjustment to living in this age of overabundance. Without lean times of food scarcity, our bodies continue to overproduce glucose, which inevitably leads to (now unnecessary) fat storage. Today insulin resistance is a health problem for many individuals.

For these insulin-resistant people, it is nearly impossible to lose weight on a low-fat, high-carbohydrate diet. Robert C. Atkins, M.D., natural medicine and mega-selling nutrition author, claims that "our bodies are just not equipped to deal with the excessive quick-energy, simple-sugar, twentieth-century diet." He believes that most people today are physically unable to process the excess glucose produced by a high-carbohydrate, high-sugar diet. "[Our] bodies overreact, causing a rapid rise in glucose, followed by its swift, prolonged fall because of an excess of insulin." Dr. Atkins advocates a low-carbohydrate diet to restore a healthy balance of blood sugar/insulin levels and to help people lose stubborn, excess pounds. Atkins notes that on a high-carbohydrate diet the body converts unused carbohydrates into glucose, which "adds fuel to the fire and upsets the sugar/insulin balance. In addition, these carbohydrates actually become addictive, resulting in a greater intake of calories."

FOOD ALLERGIES

Yet another problem with the overconsumption of carbohydrates in recent decades is the increase in often undetected allergic reactions to wheat, corn, yeast, and soy—some of the most common foods eaten on a high-carbohydrate diet. We now know that food sensitivities affect at least 60 percent of our population, yet tens of thousands of cases go undetected each year. Most people never connect their carbohydrate consumption to those last stubborn five or ten pounds they can't lose. They are unaware that a primary allergic response to eating certain carbohydrate foods is edema or water retention. People whose weight fluctuates by several pounds day to day and who often feel puffy or bloated are probably suffering unknowingly from allergy-triggered edema. I have found that once the troublesome carbohydrate is identified and eliminated from their diets, most individuals can usually get rid of their excess water and stabilize at a healthy weight.

Gluten intolerance is also the cause of many serious health problems in our carbo-loading society. An inability to digest the gluten protein found predominantly in wheat and rye, gluten intolerance is a genetic problem in which the lining of the small intestine is altered so that the consumption of gluten foods interferes with the absorption of nutrients, specifically proteins, fats, carbohydrates, calcium, iron, folic acid, and vitamins D and K. Diseases involving immune dysfunction, such as multiple sclerosis and lupus, have been studied for their possible connection to gluten intolerance.

THE KEY IS BALANCE

All of this is not to imply that carbohydrates do not have a place in a well-balanced, healthy diet. The key to the equation is *balance*. The carbohydrate craze of the last decade has sent the metabolisms of many people into a severe imbalance which now must be rectified. Even the long-held belief that high-performance athletes must "carbo-load" is now under serious scrutiny and is rapidly being replaced by scientific studies which show that athletes receive significant performance benefits from a diet balanced between protein, carbohydrates, and fat, rather than one chock-full of carbohydrates. Nutritional studies are now revealing that the optimal diet for energy production and fat burning should follow a target plan of approximately 40 percent carbohydrates, 30 percent protein, and 30 percent fats. High performance athletes may need higher carbohydrates, up to 55 percent, and less protein.

The principles of this basic regimen are gaining support from top athletes and coaches as the best plan for high performance and maximum fat burning. Massimo Testa, an Italian physician who works extensively with racing cyclists, believes that fat metabolism is the key to improving physical performance. "You need good fat burning for the aerobic engine," he says. "But the key to building a fat-burning system is to include the right fats in the diet. In Europe, we eat more fats than

Americans do, without the problem of heart disease that is seen in America."

Generally speaking, carbohydrates play a key role in dietary needs, but it is important to be well informed about the wide and varied choices of carbohydrates available. Technically, both a sugary, highly refined pastry and a plate of steamed brown rice with broccoli can be termed carbohydrates. A simple example, to be sure, yet how many of us munch on high-glycemic bagels and muffins regularly, reassuring ourselves that we are just fulfilling our daily carbo requirement? Although whole fruits and vegetables technically become carbohydrates when processed through the body, the slow-acting nature of their low-glycemic makeup, coupled with their rich nutritional profile, make fruits and vegetables the most attractive of all complex carbohydrates.

New research has shown that vegetables and fruits contain trace elements called *phytochemicals* that form a plant's immune system and act to keep the human immune system strong as well. In just a single serving of vegetables, over one-hundred different phytochemicals may be present to help ward off disease. Phytochemicals like lycopenes, for example, found in tomatoes, are powerful antioxidants that may help to prevent prostate cancer. As we will see in the following chapter, antioxidants which combat free radical damage are some of the most important elements for overall health in the human body from head to toe. Phytochemicals found in garlic and onions have been proven to lower harmful LDL cholesterol and deter the formation of cholesterol plaque deposits. Other examples include the cancer-protecting indoles found in the cruciferous family of vegetables like cabbage, Brussels sprouts, and kale.

Plant-based hormones, known as phytoestrogens, in soybeans and flax can help to prevent breast cancer in women. Phyto-chemicals in green tea, known as polyphenols, can help to pro-tect the heart.

Awareness of the type of carbohydrates you are consuming is absolutely critical. It is essential to exercise on a regular basis and cut back on highly processed, high-glycemic carbohy-drates, opting instead for low-glycemic vegetables, fruits, and whole grains. In this way, you can be assured of minimizing fat-promoting insulin production, maximizing fat-burning glucagon production, and achieving steady, balanced blood sugar levels.

CHAPTER FOUR

The Cholesterol Hoax

CHOLESTEROL! THE VERY WORD strikes fear in the hearts of most Americans. High LDLs! Run to your nearest margarine tub! Avoid eggs like the plague! Nearly anyone who has read a newspaper in the past twenty years can tell you that being diagnosed with high cholesterol feels like walking around with a time bomb ticking in the chest. Thus, they are constantly monitoring their HDL/LDL ratios and have switched to Egg Beaters and Promise to tame their unruly cholesterol levels.

In fact, many Americans—and their cardiologists—are so solely fixated on lowering cholesterol to prevent heart attack that they overlook the more potent risk factors like elevated homocysteine (a potentially toxic amino acid) and extremely depressed magnesium levels. I wonder, sometimes, if the people who are walking around scared half to death of cholesterol actually know what it is, and that too little cholesterol, like too much, can also be detrimental to health.

IS ALL CHOLESTEROL REALLY BAD?

Cholesterol is a fatlike material which, at optimal levels, is essential for good health. It plays a major role in the configuration of the sterol ring—a highly complex system which supports the adrenal and sex hormones and the entire nervous system. The body manufactures about 1,500 mg of cholesterol per day. Without enough cholesterol through dietary sources, the liver would simply manufacture it on its own. As is becoming clear, balance is critical. Too much blood cholesterol is not healthy, but neither is too little. Just as high levels of cholesterol are considered risk factors, the danger of too little cholesterol is just as real—and far less likely to receive any media attention. Cholesterol levels that fall far below 180 mg/dl may indicate anemia, acute infection, and excess thyroid function. Significantly depressed cholesterol levels have been found in patients suffering from autoimmune disorders. Low cholesterol levels have also been correlated with impaired immunity and cancer.

Cholesterol is such an important substance that it is contained in practically every cell in the human body and used for many essential functions. It helps the body manufacture adrenal hormones and sex hormones in both males and females. It also aids in the manufacture of the bile acids needed for the digestion of fat. Two-thirds of the dry weight of the brain is composed of cholesterol. Cholesterol also forms a protective coating around the myelin sheaths of the nerves and acts as a lubricant in the artery walls, reducing friction in blood flow.

Cholesterol is carried through the bloodstream in two protein components, high-density lipoprotein (HDL) and low-density lipoprotein (LDL). The HDL is considered "good" cholesterol because it carries cholesterol away from the arterial walls to the liver for disposal, thus preventing the buildup of cholesterol in the blood vessels. LDL, on the other hand, is considered harmful since it deposits cholesterol in the arterial walls, producing hardening of the arteries.

We know that elevated levels of LDL blood cholesterol are believed to be indicators of a higher risk of heart disease. We look for healthy ratios of three to one between total serum cholesterol and HDL cholesterol to reassure us of our heart health. And we avoid eggs, red meat, and other high-cholesterol foods to keep the devil cholesterol at bay. Unfortunately, the major dietary and nutritional organizations that control research and disseminate results have bought into the theory that dietary cholesterol and saturated fats raise blood cholesterol, which leads to heart disease and, ultimately, death. The only trouble is it's not true!

While cholesterol has received a bad rap, there is no solid evidence to support the case against it. Cholesterol consumption has remained essentially the same for nearly 100 years, *while heart disease rates have skyrocketed*. The consumption of animal fat has declined, *while heart disease rates have skyrocketed*. Cholesterol levels are either normal or low in half of heart disease patients. Moreover, many heart-healthy ethnic groups consume cholesterol-rich food in quantities far greater than most Americans do, yet *American heart disease rates have skyrocketed.*

In the now famous Framingham study, researchers followed the residents of Framingham, Massachusetts, for over thirty years. Initially designed to explore the correlating risk factors in the development of heart disease, the study revealed that cigarette smoking, hypertension, and diabetes were all strongly linked to heart disease. Obesity, inactivity, and a Type A personality were also shown to contribute to increased risk. What the Framingham researchers were unable to prove was a connection between diet and heart disease—specifically between eggs, meat, fat, and heart disease, although you would never know this given the intense media campaign against eggs over the last twenty years! Maybe, just maybe, other factors are involved in producing high levels of blood cholesterol.

Since the findings of the Framingham study, we now know that almost 75 percent of the cholesterol in the blood is produced by the liver, while only 25 percent is derived from foods.

THE HOMOCYSTEINE THEORY

In a recent interview in *Nature's Impact* magazine, Kilmer S. McCully, M.D., author of the groundbreaking book *The Homocysteine Revolution*, states that "investigators have shown that LDL by itself is not damaging. But when it's taken up into the artery wall, it becomes oxidized or modified, and it has damaging effects on cells in the artery wall." Dr. McCully's fascinating research into the nature and cause of heart disease has revealed the role that the amino acid homocysteine plays in LDL buildup and heart disease. Dr. McCully further notes that "food processing causes a deficiency of important B vitamins, namely B_6, B_{12}, and folic acid. These nutritional deficiencies lead to a buildup of homocysteine, an amino acid which causes heart disease."

Homocysteine buildup becomes particularly toxic when it transforms into homocysteine thiolactone. Homocysteine thiolactone and LDL cholesterol are a dangerous mix that acts in concert to damage artery walls and create plaque buildup. Dr. McCully advocates the consumption of B vitamins and folic acid to ensure against this dangerous mix. B vitamins and folic acid are able to transform homocysteine into methionine, a safe, essential amino acid, rather than allowing it to develop into homocysteine thiolactone.

FREE RADICALS AND OXIDATION

Now we know that cholesterol in and of itself is not toxic in any way, shape, or form. It is an essential component in the functioning of a healthy human body. Like a scapegoat unable to defend itself, it has been blamed for a whole host of cardiovascular problems when it is, in fact, merely an innocent bystander. Well, if cholesterol is so innocent, what *is* to blame?

Researchers now believe what many nutritionists have known for years: The process of oxidation is what makes the LDL component of cholesterol so harmful. Oxidation is a process in which fats and oils, left exposed or subjected to heat sources, interact with oxygen and create unstable atoms known as free radicals, which alter cell membranes.

Free radicals are highly reactive molecular fragments in search of stability. Constantly in search of electrons, they try to attract these electrons from other molecules, creating a chain reaction that damages cells. Environmental pollutants such as smog, cigarette smoke, X rays, chemicals, automobile exhaust, and heavy metals create these free radicals which wreak havoc on our cells, destroying tissue wherever they can. Premature aging, heart disease, cancer, and other degenerative processes are the result of rampant free radicals at work.

According to a 1979 study by Dr. C. B. Taylor in the *American Journal of Nutrition*, it is not pure cholesterol that creates artery-clogging plaque, but rather the free radicals produced by the oxidation of cholesterol. Oxidized cholesterol from food sources that have been left out at room temperature or have been fried, smoked, cured, or aged are highly atherogenic (plaque producing). Powdered, dehydrated egg and milk products found in many processed foods, and convenience items such as prepackaged gravy, instant cocoa, and soup mixes also contain oxidized cholesterol and should be avoided. These very foods also raise homocysteine levels. Fresh eggs and meats *do not* contain harmful, oxidized cholesterol, and there is no reason to avoid these products if you are attempting to eat a heart-healthy diet!

Unsaturated fats and oils are more sensitive to oxygen and therefore more quickly oxidized into free radicals than their saturated counterparts. This is a result of the double-bond chemical composition of unsaturates. Polyunsaturates contain multiple double-bonds and are even more susceptible to oxidation since they have more potential sites to which oxygen can attach. The polyunsaturates are more likely to become oxidized (with free radicals) than either the saturates or monounsaturates. The more unsaturated an oil is, the quicker it can succumb to oxidation and create free radicals.

While oxidation is a function of an oil's exposure to oxygen, heat can also play a major role in accelerating the process. Refrigerated oils do not oxidize as quickly as oils left out at room temperature. Heated oils oxidize very rapidly. At frying temperatures (300+ degrees) polyunsaturates oxidize almost immediately and become dangerous transfats.

In the American diet, most of the fat intake comes from heat-damaged, oxidized fats. In fast-food restaurants, foods are fried and the oil reused throughout the day. These foods are a perfect example of heat-damaged, oxidized fats. Because polyunsaturates are more susceptible to oxygen than saturated fats, they turn rancid more quickly and contain more free radicals. The free radicals formed by the rancid polyunsaturates attack cell membranes, enzymes, and DNA.

Nature created foods that combine the mono- and polyunsaturates with antioxidants such as vitamin E and lecithin, which combat the process of oxidation and rancidity. Unfortunately, the refining processes that food manufacturers employ strip the oils of these protective antioxidants. Polyunsaturates can also create free radicals inside the body, especially when in contact with environmental pollutants, destroying tissue wherever they can. Free radical damage continues unchecked until free radicals are neutralized by antioxidants that pair up their electrons.

Recently, researchers at the University of Texas Southwestern Medical Center, Dallas, found that a diet high in vitamin C, vitamin E, and beta carotene could help prevent further damage of heart disease. These antioxidants help prevent LDL cholesterol from oxidizing and halt the process of plaque buildup in arterial walls. To protect your body against free radical damage, take appropriate doses of antioxidants such as vitamins E and C, beta carotene, and selenium. These antioxidants, along with your body's own enzymes, combat the progress of free radical damage and are especially important in counteracting the atherogenic effect of LDL cholesterol.

IN DEFENSE OF EGGS

Eggs are without a doubt one of the most nutritious food sources known to man, and yet all the hype about dietary cholesterol and heart disease has nearly run the poor egg out of town—and the egg farmers, too, I might add.

Once and for all, I would like to set the record straight about eggs. A *germative* food, eggs contain all the essentials for growth. Their high cholesterol content is largely modified by their high levels of lecithin, actually a cholesterol-lowering agent. Lecithin, also known as *phosphatidylcholine*, is an essential element in every human cell. Acting as a protector to the cells in the nervous system, it also serves as the primary source of choline, a precursor to acetylcholine, one of the body's most valuable neurotransmitters.

Lecithin is also a natural emulsifier, which means it helps liquefy fat inside the blood vessels and prevents plaque buildup from blocking the arteries. Containing a near-perfect composition of amino acids, eggs actually provide the raw materials needed by the body to make its own antioxidants. Glutathione, one of the antioxidants formed by an amino acid provided by eggs, actually helps all the other antioxidants in the body to slow cancer, prevent cataracts, and *prevent the oxidation of LDL cholesterol.*

Some egg farmers are now producing eggs that are also high in omega-3 fatty acids. Using feed enriched with omega-3 oils, egg producers such as The Country Hen, Born "3," and Pilgrim's Pride Eggs Plus have developed eggs enriched with these healthy oils. According to *The Omega Plan*, by Artemis P. Simopoulos, M.D., "In small studies, eating two omega-3 enriched eggs a day did not cause a rise in LDL cholesterol. In addition, it lowered triglycerides and raised HDL cholesterol."

TRANSFATS

By now, I hope I have convinced you that cholesterol is not the demon it has been made out to be. I would now like to introduce you to a type of fat that I do believe is a nutritional devil, one that should be avoided as much as possible.

Heat-damaged fats, like the fats in fried foods, have been transformed by high temperatures into "transfats," unnatural man-made fats that, among other things, interfere with the body's ability to efficiently process good fat into essential hormones and lubricants.

Many commercially processed oils are now labeled "hydrogenated." This means they have been chemically processed for the manufacturers' benefit (they have a longer shelf life). Shortening is a prime example of a hydrogenated fat. In creating shortening or margarine, manufacturers must heat vegetable oil to very high temperatures and then artificially bond hydrogen atoms into the gaps in the oil's carbon chains. This hydrogenation fills the unsaturated oil's gaps, effectively rendering it saturated and solid. Unfortunately, and this is critical to understand, forcing a vegetable oil through the process of hydrogenation transforms it from a natural, healthy oil into a hazardous, saturated transfat. Contrary to what the marketing mavens would have us believe, margarine is a prime example of a hazardous transfat.

Transfats, Breast Cancer, and Heart Disease

Transfats are found in many processed and fast foods, most margarines, and some vegetable oils. In a study published in September 1997 of nearly 700 postmenopausal women in Europe, researchers at the University of North Carolina found that women whose body fat registered the highest levels of transfatty acids were up to 40 percent more prone to develop breast cancer than research participants with low transfat levels. The study also revealed that a combination of high transfat intake and low polyunsaturate intake was particularly dangerous to women's health. The tendency to develop breast cancer was found to be almost three-and-a-half times as high among women with both high transfatty acid levels and low levels of polyunsaturated fatty acids than in women with low transfat intake. This study has particular and frightening relevance for American women since we, on average, consume almost twice as much transfat as European women.

Supporting this September 1997 research are the recently published results of the Nurses' Health Study. Following 80,000 nurses for fourteen years, this study reported on the effects of all dietary fats in women. Harvard researchers recently reported that it is the type of fats consumed, not the total amount of fat, which determines a woman's risk of suffering a heart attack. The fourteen-year Nurses' Health Study identified two types of fats as particularly harmful in contributing to heart disease: saturated fats (found in meat and dairy foods) and transfats (found in margarines as well as processed bakery products and foods fried with hydrogenated vegetable oils). In contrast to earlier research, which focused mainly on total fat and cholesterol levels, the new findings confirm the risks associated with the transfats. While considering other risk factors involved in coronary heart disease like smoking, transfats stood out as the most potent hazard. Among the women in the study who consumed the highest amount of transfats, the chance of suffering a heart attack was found to be 53 percent higher than those who had a low transfat intake. Researchers said they believed the dangers of transfats would hold up in future research for both men and women.

In addition, the Nurses' Health Study revealed that the amount of total fat consumed has little bearing on the relative risk of suffering a heart attack. Women with the highest consumption of total fat (46 percent of calories) were found to be at no greater risk of heart attack than those with the lowest fat intake (29 percent of calories).

Metabolic studies show that although saturated fats raise the level of "bad" LDL cholesterol, transfats not only raise LDL but also lower the levels of the "good" HDL cholesterol. Transfats were also found to raise the level of triglycerides, another form of blood fat associated with heart disease.

Dr. Frank Hu, the lead researcher of the study, noted that "the best solution is to decrease saturated fats and avoid transfats. Replace unhealthy fats with healthy ones—monounsaturates and polyunsaturates from natural vegetable oils." Researchers from the Harvard School of Public Health concluded that this study suggested that *limiting consumption of transfats would be more effective in avoiding heart attacks than reducing overall fat intake.*

Unfortunately, transfats are not listed on food labels. I believe this is a gross injustice to the American public. So, when shopping the aisles of your local supermarket, you need to know what to avoid. A product is likely to contain transfats if hydrogenated fat is listed among the ingredients. Check carefully; most commercially prepared baked goods, even sliced breads, contain hydrogenated oils. As a general rule, the softer (or more liquid) the oil, the fewer transfats it contains. Try to buy foods with fats that have not been altered from their natural state. Remember that oils are naturally liquid; butter is naturally solid.

Natural fats like butter and other animal fats are more easily broken down by the body than transfats. Natural fats provide the body's most important energy source and contain some important vitamins and nutrients. The body uses these animal fats as necessary; they provide protective cushioning around the vital organs.

BUTTER IS BETTER

By now you may be saying to yourself: First she tells me eggs are healthy, then she says that margarine is hazardous, next she'll be saying I shouldn't be wary of butter. Well, you've got that right!

While I don't advocate overconsumption of butter just as I don't advocate overconsumption of any food or nutrient, I am not alone in my belief that butter has been unfairly demonized in the last half of this century. In a 1995 article in *Health Freedom News*, Mary Enig, Ph.D., and Sally Fallon, M.A., explain that "between 1920 and 1960, the incidence of heart disease rose precipitously to become America's number-one killer. During the same period, butter consumption plummeted from eighteen pounds per year to four pounds per year. It doesn't take a Ph.D. in statistics to conclude butter is not a cause. Actually butter contains many nutrients that protect us from heart disease."

Like eggs, butter contains lecithin, which aids in the metabolic breakdown of cholesterol. It is also a rich source of vitamin A, which is necessary for the healthy functioning of the adrenal and thyroid glands. The vitamins A and E and the mineral selenium in butter also serve as important antioxidants in protecting against free radical damage that can destroy tissues and weaken arterial walls.

Enig and Fallon go on to explain that the wholesale abandonment of butter in recent decades was accelerated by early research which "indicated that increased fat intake caused cancer." They note that the press "neglected to stress the fact that the saturated fats used in these experiments were not naturally saturated fats, but partially hydrogenated or hardened fats— the kind found mostly in margarine but *not in butter*"(italics mine). In an ironic twist, butter was unfairly portrayed as the villain by the media, while the true culprits (hydrogenated transfats like those found in margarines) were elevated as heart-healthy heroes!

Butter, most animal fats, and tropical vegetable fats are solid at room temperature while most other vegetable oils are liquid or semiliquid. This is because animal fats and butter are "saturated." We've all been warned repeatedly about the dangers of saturated fats, but natural saturated fats are beginning to be recognized for their vital, protective qualities. While it is important to limit excess consumption of saturated fats because of their artery-clogging capabilities, a balanced diet should contain a limited amount of saturated fats for their organ-protective function.

THE HEART-HEALTHY FATS

In 1960, the important "Seven Countries Study" revealed that men on the Greek island of Crete "were healthier than all the other 12,000 men surveyed in seven quite different countries—Greece, Italy, the Netherlands, Finland, Yugoslavia, Japan, and the United States." The men in Crete had half the number of cancer mortalities and one-twentieth the amount of terminal coronary heart disease of American men. And even though the Cretan diet, at over 35 percent fat, contained nearly three times more fat than the Japanese diet, the men in Crete had half the overall death rate from degenerative diseases of Japanese men. The best guess of researchers at the time was that the health of the men in Crete was somehow attributable to the lower saturated fat and higher olive oil content of their diet. Little was known back then about the heart-healthy effects of the omega oils and the importance of balancing the intake of omega fats.

In 1994, this "best guess" became a proven fact, thanks to the landmark Lyon Diet Heart Study conducted in France by Michel de Lorgeril, Serge Renaud, and J. Delaye. Over 600 French patients recovering from heart attacks were placed on either the American Heart Association (AHA) "prudent diet" or on a modified "Crete" diet, in which canola oil was used as the major source of omega-3 alpha linolenic acid. The Crete-styled diet was over 35 percent fat, while the AHA diet was 30 percent fat. In her 1998 book *The Omega Plan*, Artemis Simopoulos notes that "just four months into the trial, the researchers discovered there had been significantly fewer deaths in the group with the modified Crete diet than on the AHA diet." After following their subjects for two years, the researchers suddenly decided to terminate the study. The new Crete diet, with its optimal balance of omega-3 and omega-6 oils, was so clearly preferable it would have been unethical to continue keeping the control group on the AHA diet. In contrast to patients on the AHA diet, the subjects on the Crete diet had a whopping 76 percent lower risk of suffering from a heart attack, heart failure, stroke, or dying from cardiovascular disease!

In another thought-provoking twist to traditional thinking, the heart-protective effects of the Crete diet were not related to the patients' blood levels of LDL, HDL, or total cholesterol. Even though the patients on the Crete diet were avoiding heart attacks, strokes, and death far better than their AHA counterparts, their serum cholesterol levels were essentially equal to those in the AHA control group. When researchers looked back to verify this, they found that the men from Crete in the "Seven Countries Study" never had serum cholesterol levels in the "desirable" range (under 180 mg/dl) even when they were in the best of health. As older men of seventy to eighty-nine, their cholesterol levels averaged around 220, yet they had become very healthy, vital older men, thanks to the optimal balance of omega-3 and omega-6 oils in their diet.

Another now famous study of the Eskimo community also confirmed the benefits of omega oils in reducing the occurrence of heart disease. Members of the Eskimo community were found to have a very low incidence of coronary heart disease despite their diet of extremely high fat. Researchers found that the fat the Eskimos were eating was the "good" fat found in fish rich in the omega-3 fatty acids. Deep cold-water fish such as cod, herring, salmon, trout, sardines, mackerel, and tuna all contain oils rich in the omega-3 oils of eicosapentaenoic acid (EPA) and docosahexaenoic acid (DHA).

We now know that the omega-3 oils DHA and EPA both contribute to a decreased risk of blood clots. Blocked arteries form when blood platelets become sticky and clump together. These "clumps" clog arteries and block the flow of blood throughout the system. EPA works to prevent blood platelets from becoming "sticky" and blocking blood flow. It also aids in reversing the inflammatory processes that lead to cardiovascular disease and prevents the rupturing of blood membranes that can clot and cause strokes.

When subjects in one study who were suffering with high blood levels of fats and cholesterol were given fish oil supplements, their elevated levels of fat and cholesterol *returned to normal*. Not only do the omega fats not raise cholesterol levels, they actually work to normalize them and promote healthy blood functioning. Furthermore, some of the more recent research suggests that omega-3s prevent blood clotting, repair tissue damage caused by clogged arteries, lower the rate at which the liver makes triglycerides, lower high blood pressure, and protect the body from autoimmune diseases.

Essential fatty acids are truly good bets for a healthy heart. A healthy balance of the heart-smart omega oils can help lower cholesterol, lower triglycerides, and protect against heart disease by making the blood thinner, less sticky, and less likely to clot.

CHAPTER FIVE

The Protein Power Connection

T HE PERCENTAGE OF PROTEIN in the average American diet has dropped precipitously in recent decades, an unhealthy result of both the carbohydrate craze and the cholesterol hoax. Attempting to regulate unruly cholesterol levels, many Americans swore off red meat, eggs, and dairy products in the 1970s and 1980s, eliminating many of the best sources of complete proteins from their diets in the process. Compounding this rejection of high-protein foods was all the media attention in recent years that suggested that a diet high in carbohydrates and low in all fats was the absolute healthiest way to go.

As we now know, high LDL serum cholesterol levels are the result of oxidized fats, transfats, and damage caused by free radicals. Although I believe it is wise to stay away from fatty meats, there is no sound dietary reason to avoid lean meats, eggs, and low-fat dairy products. Quite the contrary! As we saw in chapter 3, in their attempt to fulfill the low-fat, high-carbohydrate dictates of the last decade, Americans have been turning in droves away from protein-rich foods, reaching instead for refined, high-glycemic carbohydrates like pasta and bagels. This has resulted in weight gain, fatigue, and, in many cases, illness and disease. I believe that the low-fat, high-carbohydrate craze of the 1980s has translated directly into the physical deterioration of the 1990s.

People I know feel almost virtuous when they reduce the amount of protein in their diet. Believing that low protein equals low fat, many clients I meet think that the lower the protein content in their diet, the healthier they will be. Nothing could be further from the truth. A person suffering from protein deficiency can experience significant physical and emotional illness and malnutrition. Fatigue, confusion, irritability, and a decreased libido, as well as dry skin, brittle nails, and hair loss are all signs of a lack of protein in the diet.

When you aren't consuming enough protein, you battle intense cravings, often for foods high in simple sugars. When it seems like a candy bar is all you really need, your body actually may be starving for protein. Protein, like healthy fat, has a stabilizing effect on blood sugar and provides the body with the long-lasting, steady energy it demands. Sugar cravings are merely the body's way of looking for foods that will provide it with quick, easily metabolized energy. Unfortunately, as we discovered in chapter 3, giving in to the sugar craving will result in a sugar rush followed by a crash in energy level and a continuous craving for more sugar.

As a rule, whenever I meet a client with a craving for sweets, I immediately ask about his or her protein intake. If *your* protein intake is low and you find yourself craving sweets, try increasing your daily protein intake. I recommend a moderate amount of protein balanced with some healthy fat—tuna fish or a hard-boiled egg with canola mayonnaise, for example.

Increasing protein intake will eliminate sugar cravings and boost energy levels significantly.

WHAT IS PROTEIN?

Protein is comprised of twenty-two amino acids that maintain and protect muscle cells and all the vital organs as well as the blood, skin, and connective tissues. Nine of the amino acids are essential, which means they must be obtained from dietary sources because the body cannot manufacture them on its own.

The Nine Essential Amino Acids

Histidine Found primarily in meats, poultry, eggs, and certain cheeses, histidine is essential for the production of red and white blood cells. Adequate supplies of histidine regenerate and repair body tissue. Histidine is also a precursor of the neurotransmitter, histamine, which is active in immune response.

Isoleucine Isoleucine is plentiful in meats, eggs, poultry, cheeses, and certain fish. One of the three "stress amino acids," isoleucine is necessary for hemoglobin and energy production.

Leucine Meats, cheeses, poultry, and wheat germ are all wonderful sources of leucine. Another "stress amino acid," leucine is located primarily in lean muscle tissue. Fundamental for growth, leucine supports bone, muscle, and skin development by triggering specific protein syntheses.

Lysine Along with meats, poultry, fish, eggs, and cheeses, lysine is also plentiful in legumes. Lysine is particularly important for skin and bone health. It promotes the development of healthy collagen, skin, and bone and enables the body to efficiently process calcium.

Methionine Vegetarians need to ensure adequate methionine consumption, since this amino acid is quite low in most legumes, including soybeans. Meats, eggs, cheeses, and many seeds and nuts contain healthy levels of methionine, which is a sulfur-based amino acid. Methionine is critical to fat metabolism and acts as an antioxidant for the entire physical system.

Phenylalanine This amino acid is critical for healthy brain functioning. Found in meats, eggs, certain cheeses, and wheat germ, phenylalanine plays an important role in the development of neurotransmitters. Studies have proven that phenylalanine acts as an effective antidepressant and painkiller in the brain.

Threonine Rich in meat, eggs, and beans, threonine is particularly low in grain-based foods. Essential for healthy immune system functioning, threonine also promotes skin, bone, and tooth enamel production and supports the healthy functioning of the thymus gland.

Tryptophan A precursor to serotonin, the neurotransmitter that affects mood and sleep functioning, tryptophan is found primarily in meats, poultry (especially turkey), certain cheeses, and nuts. Grains and legumes are a poor source of tryptophan.

Valine Found in meats, poultry, eggs, cheeses, and wheat germ, valine is the third "stress amino acid." Essential for energy production, valine impacts growth hormones and body metabolism.

Animal protein, like that found in lean beef, poultry, fish, and eggs, contains all the amino acids required by the human body. The protein in animal products is described as complete since one serving provides each of the nine essential amino acids. Nonanimal protein is labeled incomplete, because no vegetable or grain is able to provide each of the nine essential amino acids on its own. However, as most vegetarians know, it is possible to combine these foods within the course of a day to produce a vegetarian diet that provides complete protein with all nine essential amino acids.

The body cannot function without all of the necessary amino acids. If one of the nonessential amino acids is in short supply, the body will simply manufacture more. However, if the body is deficient in one of the nine essential amino acids, it will begin cannibalizing its own muscle tissue to extract the necessary amino acids. This is the worst thing that could happen to the body's metabolism.

LEAN PROTEIN IS A METABOLIC ACTIVATOR

In an attempt to lose body fat, many women and men cut back severely on their protein intake. While they may recognize the poor muscle tone and loss of muscle mass that often result from protein insufficiency, many do not realize that cutting back on protein intake only serves to destroy their fat-burning, lean muscle tissue.

The higher the percentage of lean muscle, the faster the metabolism will be and the more calories will be burned on a daily basis. Protein is absolutely essential for building muscle and boosting the rate at which the body burns stored fat. In fact, the only way to build lean muscle mass is by eating sufficient quantities of protein.

The less lean muscle a person has, the harder it is to burn fat and calories. With loss of muscle mass comes a drastic slowing of the metabolic rate and an increase in the rate of fat storage. Thus, insufficient protein intake equals a loss of muscle mass, a slowed metabolism, and an increase in the body's propensity to store fat. To prevent loss of lean muscle mass it is essential to consume adequate amounts of complete protein. If you've never been concerned about maintaining healthy stores of lean muscle tissue, take note: The more muscle mass you have, the *faster your metabolism will be* and the *faster you will burn fat* and calories.

PROTEIN POWER

One of the most important roles of protein is to stimulate the pancreas to produce the hormone glucagon. As I detailed in chapter 3, glucagon's primary function is to unlock your stored fat cells for use as energy. You will recall that with too much insulin in the body, glucagon is literally blocked from unlocking stores of fat, and the body is unable to burn its own fat.

In this scenario, protein acts in the reverse of insulin. When a person eats adequate quantities of protein (especially in combination with healthy fats and low sugar), the pancreas produces the right amount of glucagon to mobilize stored body fat so the body can begin burning excess fat for energy.

Protein strengthens the immune system by aiding in the production of antibodies, the body's armies against disease. Antibodies are essential for fighting illnesses brought on by infection, viruses, and bacteria. If protein intake is insufficient, the production of antibodies will suffer. If the body is deficient in antibodies, the immune system is compromised, resulting in increased susceptibility to colds, flu, infections, or worse. Proteins also act to promote healthy immune functioning at the cellular level. Instrumental in the function of leukocytes and lymphocytes, protein helps maintain the body's healthy cellular metabolic rate and resistance to bacteria and other invaders. If untreated for too long, protein deficiency can result in liver disease and anemia.

Critical in the development of tissue growth and healing, protein also plays a crucial role in the formation of neurotransmitters in the brain. It helps the body create new cells to replace those that die off every day. Without enough protein, healthy new cells will not be formed—the skin will be thin and dry, the hair fragile with a tendency to fall out, and the nails brittle. If you currently recognize any of these symptoms in yourself, check your protein intake.

A lesser known function of protein is its role in maintaining fluid balance in the body. Proteins in blood attract molecules of water, controlling the water levels between cells, within cells, and within your arteries and veins. When the body is deficient in protein, the fluid in the cells cannot be drawn in by the blood and will not be efficiently eliminated by the kidneys. Thus, a diet low in protein will actually result in water retention, water weight gain, and uncomfortable bloating.

As noted earlier, protein can boost metabolic rate by helping the body build lean muscle mass. It also acts as a wonderful source of ongoing, steady energy throughout the day. If you feel tired and sluggish on a regular basis, check your protein levels. Chances are you're not getting enough protein in your diet. Adding lean meats and poultry will leave you with more energy and fewer energy swings throughout your day.

Eating healthy amounts of meats, fish, and poultry, especially in combination with essential fatty acids, will jump-start the body's ability to burn excess fat. While a high-carbohydrate meal boosts metabolic rate by about 4 percent, a high-protein meal raises metabolism about 30 percent. Lean proteins and essential fatty acids equal fat burning, not fat storage.

HOW MUCH IS ENOUGH?

Now that you understand why a diet with adequate protein levels is critical, you may be wondering how much protein you should be taking in. Experts disagree on how much protein is necessary for human health. However, more and more research is showing that a diet that is 30 percent protein is optimal for health and an efficient fuel-burning metabolism.

Thirty percent! That's way above the government recommendations of 10 percent protein in the diet (50 grams of protein in a 2,000 calorie diet). I believe that government estimates are far too low for optimal health. The government seems to have selected a percentage which, in my estimation, is the bare minimum a body requires to sustain itself. While all bodies have different needs, I believe a percentage of protein in the 25 to 35 percent range is preferable for *optimal* health. Remember, you are increasing the percentage of protein in your total diet. This means you will have to lower the percentage of another food group. When you consider that for most people such an increase in protein will take the place of calories formerly obtained from highly processed, sugary carbohydrates, the proper choice seems abundantly clear.

THE HISTORICAL IMPORTANCE OF PROTEIN

Two of the best sources of complete dietary protein, meat and eggs, have been vilified by the media in recent decades. Blamed for health problems from heart disease and high cholesterol to obesity, meat and eggs have been banished from all heart-healthy diet plans. This is a grave mistake, a mistake that is literally costing Americans their health.

Avoiding protein-rich sources like meat and eggs is not the way to avoid high cholesterol, heart disease, or obesity. As I have discussed in chapter 4, transfats have been proven to play a much more significant role in increased risk of heart disease than any other type of fat, and most high-protein sources have little to no transfats. The collective shift away from protein-rich foods toward refined sugars and processed carbohydrates has only served to increase levels of heart disease, obesity, and diabetes. We now know that high serum cholesterol levels are largely the result of oxidation and free radical damage. Avoiding oxidized meats, like those which have been cured or aged, will greatly reduce the risk of increased serum cholesterol levels from animal products.

But what about the saturated fats in beef? While I don't encourage my clients to eat fatty cuts of meat, I do believe the dangers of saturated fats have been overstated. Studies like the Nurses' Health Study give us reason to believe that transfats are significantly more hazardous to our health than animal fats. The primary problem I have with today's beef is that, unlike the grass-fed cattle of yesteryear, today's cattle is grain-fed. That grain has been laced with the growth hormone stilbesterol. As a result, much of the beef sold in supermarkets today has a high content of stearic acid, which promotes production of LDL cholesterol.

Look for beef that is "certified" and fed natural grains without antibiotics, growth stimulants, or animal by-products. Belle Brook Farms in Nacogdoches, Texas, has the most delicious natural beef I have ever tasted. It is naturally lean with no added growth stimulants or antibiotics and is genetically tender due to its finer muscle fiber. Call (409) 560-9482 for further information.

WHAT ABOUT VEGETARIANS?

What about those of you who are vegetarian? Vegatarianism is considered by many to be the healthiest and most natural lifestyle for humankind.

I, too, was once a committed vegetarian—a vegan who ate only plant foods. But it was not a healthy diet plan for me. I do believe that some people can be healthy on a vegetarian diet, but I do not advocate vegetarianism across the board. When I was vegan, my body began a slow process of deterioration. For nearly a year I ate natural, whole foods, avoided all types of animal protein, and worked hard at combining foods to ensure an adequate intake of amino acids. But I was slowly falling apart. My hair started falling out, and my skin erupted. I lost twenty pounds, and I couldn't tolerate any excess stimuli (I became especially sensitive to noise). Yet, I was committed to keeping my body free of animal products. After all, I knew the drill. I could automatically recite how the length of the human intestines and the number of molars versus incisors were phys- ical proof that humans were not designed to be meat eaters. Unfortunately, I was wrong, and my body was protesting with unmistakable signals.

Protein was important for early Paleolithic man. Early humans got most of their nourishment from fish and meat, and fruits and vegetables—just two of what we now regard as the four food groups. The proteins in meat and fish have been a critical part of the human diet for 40,000 years—an eternity for us, but for human genetics, a mere blip in the evolutionary time line. Any difference between our present genetic makeup and that of humans who lived during the Paleolithic era, a mere 40,000 to 15,000 years ago, is believed to be negligible. We have been designed to eat protein, vegetables, and essential fatty acids (in fish and many green plants that Paleolithic man con- sumed). Notice that our early ancestors were not eating the breads or dairy products we think of as so basic to our present diets. Grains and dairy products are relatively recent foodstuffs, largely the result of domestication of animals and the agricultural revolution. From the standpoint of genetically determined human biology, these foods are "Johnny-come-latelies."

With the advent of the agricultural revolution, humans started consuming more and more grain-based products and were able to harvest the dairy products of domesticated animals. As a result, protein consumption began its long, slow decline in the human diet, and carbohydrate consumption began to rise. In their book *Protein Power,* Michael and Mary Dan Eades cite research which shows that after this shift to a lower-protein, higher-carbohydrate diet, human beings began experiencing a decline in health, and degenerative diseases began to proliferate.

In my own experience, it wasn't until my parents and a nutritionally oriented physician convinced me to start eating chicken and begin taking megavitamins that I began to regain my health and physical vitality. Today, as a nutritionist who consults with hundreds of clients a year, I see men and women experiencing the same symptoms I did over and over again.

I have seen countless women who pride themselves on their ability to maintain a no-fat diet free of all animal protein, including dairy foods and eggs. They munch on lettuce, no-fat yogurt, and bagels, feeling virtuous about their ability to control their fat intake. By nightfall they are wrecks. Craving sugar (really craving the steady energy of protein and healthy fat), they reach for the low-fat, high-sugar carbohydrate snacks we know so well—cookies, frozen yogurt, and aspartame-laden soft drinks. If this cycle continues long enough, they begin to experience mood swings, edginess, depression, and physical symptoms like hair loss, water retention, fatigue, and a slowed metabolism. When I can convince them that a return to lean proteins and healthy fats will not cause them to gain weight, my clients agree to put animal protein back into their diets. Within weeks of increasing their protein intake, I invariably see metabolism levels increase, muscle tone rise, and energy levels soar.

If you are experiencing any of the symptoms described here, I urge you to begin adding more protein and essential fatty acids to your diet. Chapter 12 provides detailed menus and shopping lists for a healthy intake of protein and fatty acids.

CHAPTER SIX

Omega Fats: The Satiety Factor

F AT IS THE SATIETY NUTRIENT. It makes food taste good
and, of all the nutrients, does the best job of allowing us to
feel not only full but also satisfied after a meal.

As the most concentrated energy source (supplying 9 calories per gram), fats release the hormone cholecystokinin
(CCK) from the stomach to the brain, signaling a message of
satiety. Without that message, we continue to feel hungry and
dissatisfied after a meal. What happens when you reduce or
eliminate the satiety nutrient from your diet? Your brain does
not receive a message of satiety, and while your stomach may
be stuffed, you do not feel "satisfied."

Feeling "full, but not satisfied" on low-fat diets has left many
people questioning their bodies and the messages their bodies
are sending them. "How can I be hungry if I just ate?" "Why do
I feel like I need more food if my stomach is clearly stuffed?"
"How can I be craving ice cream when I just ate such a healthy,
low-fat meal?"

Understanding the process of satiety enables us to see why
people on low-fat diets chronically complain of feeling full but

not satisfied. They eat large quantities of food—food low in fat but not always low in calories—and are left a short while later feeling hungry. Then they reach for a low-fat snack, typically one laden with sugar and refined carbohydrates, which sends them for a ride on the glucose roller coaster described in chapter 3.

This is yet another vicious cycle that dieters become trapped in as they try to adhere to the false gospel of the fat-free diet. The body has developed finely tuned message centers to communicate all sorts of information about our physical status. When we eat even a relatively small quantity of fat, the stomach releases the hormonal CCK message to the brain, signaling both fullness and satiety. The brain receives the message and, if we are listening, we register the feeling of satisfaction and stop eating. However, if we are eating a no-fat or very low-fat diet, the stomach becomes stuffed with food without ever sending the message of fullness and satiety to the brain. The stomach is uncomfortably full, but the brain never registers a feeling of satisfaction. We are "full, yet not satisfied."

A low-fat diet actually creates a scenario in which the dieter, who believes the problem is with the body anyway, begins mistrusting the messages the body is sending: "If I'm stuffing myself with food, why do I want to keep eating?" "I guess I'm just one of those people who never feels full." "I wonder what's wrong with me?" Low-fat diets interrupt the messages your body is trying to send to your brain. If there is little or no fat being taken in, there is no hormonal message of satiety sent to the brain. Your body registers the physical feeling of fullness, but not of satisfaction. Then you get confused. You think, "There must be something wrong with me." You begin to mistrust your body and become even more alienated from the signals it tries to send. Soon you disregard all signals regarding hunger, fullness, and satiety. You listen, instead, to advertising claims and diet gurus. You forget how to listen to your own body, and soon you believe that following an external diet plan, rather than your own body's internal cues, is the only way you will ever lose weight.

When you begin to add essential fatty acids back into your diet, you enable your body to send clear messages to your brain. You eat. You are full *and* satisfied. You stop eating until you are hungry again. Depending on the amount of fat you have eaten with your meal, you usually will not feel hungry again for four to six hours. When you do get hungry, it's time to eat. Adding essential fats back into your diet encourages your body's natural process of food intake and internal regulation. This is the way your body was designed by nature to function and the only real way to maintain a healthy weight over an extended period of time.

Without consuming enough of the essential fats, your body's signals get jammed. Soon you can't rely on your body's messages. You mistrust your body and fixate on external diet plans to get you through. Convinced even more that the problem is with you, and not with what you are (or aren't) eating, you cling even more tenaciously to the "rules" of your diet and berate yourself as weak willed when you "slip."

THE CASE OF ANGIE

I remember well the case of Angie, who had lost a good deal of weight on one of the more popular diet programs. For Angie, fat was the enemy. She was on a strict program of vegetables, carbohydrates, and extra-lean meats. No fat would pass her lips. As we were talking one day, she described herself as a "volume eater." She explained that this meant she needed large amounts of food to fill her stomach. Her standard lunch and dinner was a huge bowl of steamed vegetables, a minuscule slice of skinless chicken breast, six rice cakes, and a large diet soda. She came to me to figure out why she never felt satisfied after meals and why she constantly battled the urge to binge on sugary, high-fat foods. She was upset by these "moments of weakness" and felt she had to struggle quite hard to select "healthy," fat-free good-ies (actually laden with sugar, hydrogenated oils, and refined carbohydrates) when she felt the urge to binge.

Angie's "fat phobia," born and bred in the fat-free craze of the 1980s, led to her struggles with bingeing and mistrust of her body. Yet even after she intellectually accepted the idea that essential fats could improve her health, she remained convinced that increasing her fat intake would result in weight gain.

Angie was terrified of fat. She believed eating anything with fat would immediately cause her to gain weight and/or drop dead from a heart attack. It took me months before I could convince Angie to experiment by adding some fat to her diet. She struggled hard against the idea that moderate amounts of essential fats could actually be healthy for her. Finally she agreed to try it for two weeks. Within days, Angie began to feel more satisfied after eating. As we increased the quantity of essential fats and proteins in her diet, she began to feel satisfied after eating smaller quantities of food. With the increase in fat and protein in her diet, Angie reported a dramatic decrease in her urge to binge. Angie now eats healthy, moderate quantities of essential fats, proteins, and complex carbohydrates. She no longer considers herself a volume eater and is able to feel full and satisfied with moderate amounts of food. She no longer struggles with the urge to binge and allows herself "real" desserts in small quantities from time to time. Her weight is stable and well within the healthy range for her height and age.

EATING ESSENTIAL FATS WILL NOT MAKE YOU FAT

The most common misconception about fat is that *eating fat makes you fat*. One reason so many people have been taken in by this false idea is that it has been the central theme in several best-selling diet books. Eat a high-fat diet, say a number of prominent diet doctors, and you will have a high-fat body. One has gone so far as to say: You can't get fat *except* by eating fat!

Nothing could be further from the truth. Of course, if you consume large quantities of fat without regard for your bodily requirements, you will gain weight. But, as I have stated in earlier chapters, eating the right types of essential fats actually helps the metabolism burn calories more efficiently. Eating moderate amounts of essential fats balances the body's ratio of insulin to glucagon. You will recall from chapter 3 that adequate levels of glucagon unlock the body's fat storage banks and begin converting fat into energy. Taking in moderate amounts of healthy fats also stabilizes blood sugar. As a long-lasting nutrient, fat is metabolized slowly and actually decreases the rate at which carbohydrates are released into the system, and, because it is a slow-burning nutrient, fat can keep the appetite satisfied for up to six hours at a time.

In a special report on the new evidence on fat in *Bicycling* magazine, Phillip Maffetone describes how higher levels of healthy fats are being added to the training diets of world-class athletes. In an effort to boost the fat-burning potential of his trainees, Maffetone is encouraging a plan of 40 percent carbohydrates, 30 percent protein, and 30 percent fat. This increases the fat in many athletes' regimens by 50 to 100 percent! Maffetone explains that taking in moderate amounts of fat enables the body to convert stored fat into energy. He claims "the benefits are enormous. Less fat is stored (leading to weight loss). [And] endurance is improved." Maffetone is quick to note that this plan is not only for elite performers but also for healthy adults who want to experience greater energy and an increased ability to burn fat when they exercise.

That fatty foods tend to make you fat has been overstated. In fact, you may be surprised to learn that you can *lose* weight just as effectively on a high-fat diet as a low-fat diet, provided the two diets contain the same number of calories. In a study at the University Hospital in Geneva, Switzerland, one group of patients was put on a 45 percent-fat diet, while another group was put on a 26 percent-fat diet. Although the fat content varied dramatically, both diets contained a low 1,200 calories. At the end of the three-month study, both groups had lost equal amounts of weight. One concludes that an ideal diet contains a *moderate* amount of healthy fat and that eating fat *in and of itself* will not make you fat.

The medical establishment, including doctors, nurses, dietitians, and nutritionists, have all swallowed the decree of low fat/no fat "hook, line, and sinker." While the establishment authorities applaud the national reduction of fat intake from more than 40 percent of total calories to 33 percent—the inescapable consequences are that in the last ten years, 20 million people in the United States became obese and the number of obese children doubled, all the while seemingly reducing the percentage of fat in their diets. Perhaps fat wasn't the enemy after all.

BECOMING FAT FRIENDLY

This notion of fat as essential to health and well-being is currently being promoted by what was once the voice of the fat-free goddess: women's magazines. Several years after I wrote *Beyond Pritikin* (which makes the case of good versus bad fats quite dramatically), women's magazines are finally getting on the "not all fat is bad for you" bandwagon. A healthy and essential fat-based diet now represents a new approach to dieting.

While I am glad these magazines are promoting the idea that fat is no longer a dietary demon, I must admit I find calling it a "new approach" somewhat amusing, considering the fact that I wrote *Beyond Pritikin* in 1988!

Adding essential fats into your diet actually encourages weight loss by promoting the feeling of fullness and satiety. You are satisfied for longer periods of time—up to six hours—and you don't need to be constantly munching on no-fat foods like high-glycemic pretzels and rice cakes in an attempt to calm the nagging hunger in your already full stomach.

Putting essential fats back into the diet returns the body to a natural, healthy state in which the stomach can communicate with the brain. When your stomach is comfortably full, you will also feel calmly satisfied. You will not be constantly searching for something to pop into your mouth. While this idea may sound new and exciting to you, it is as old as humankind itself. It is the way nature designed our bodies to function.

CHAPTER SEVEN

Omega Fats:
The Fat-burning Value

T HERE ARE TWO TYPES OF FAT CELLS in the body: white fat
and brown fat. White fat is the insulating layer of fat just
beneath the skin that keeps us warm and supplies us with fat
for energy during lean times. Brown fat, on the other hand, lies
deep within the body, surrounding vital organs such as the
heart, kidneys, and adrenal glands. It cushions the spinal col-
umn as well as the neck and major thoracic blood vessels.

The name "brown fat" is deceptive, since brown fat differs so
greatly from the white fat that we battle against so ferociously.
Brown fat is the opposite of white fat in that it is not storage
fat. Brown fat is a completely unique type of fat that *burns*
calories for heat rather than retaining those calories for future
use. A calorie-burning engine efficiently converting calories
into heat, brown fat makes it possible to expend ingested fat as
energy rather than storing it as excess white fat.

Uncovering the complex processes of brown fat will go a
long way in helping to understand why some people remain
slim regardless of their consumption of excess calories while

others gain weight easily, as if their bodies immediately store any caloric excess as fat.

Discovered by researchers investigating the process of adaptation to cold, brown fat serves the body in two distinct ways. One function of brown fat is its role in adapting the body to cold climates; the other is its role in weight control. Brown fat is comprised of numerous fat-burning cells that contain large quantities of mitochondria, which actually give the fat its brown color. The mitochondria work day and night converting fat calories into usable heat energy. White fat, on the other hand, contains few mitochondria and is retained by the body for future use. Researchers have discovered that thin people who have little trouble managing extra calories have activated mitochondria in their brown fat, while overweight individuals have dormant brown fat. Brown fat levels decrease with age, which may be why some adults tend to gain weight as they age.

The body employs brown fat to convert calories into heat energy via the process of thermogenesis, which takes place in many of the body's cells. However, it is only in brown fat that thermogenesis is the primary function. Although brown fat makes up 10 percent or less of total body fat, it is responsible for 25 percent of all the fat calories burned by all the other body tissues combined.

Brown fat, when signaled by the brain to begin its work, burns excess calories rapidly and efficiently. All too often, however, the body's fat-burning engine does not work properly. When this occurs, thermogenesis does not take place, and the body resorts to its fall-back position—storing excess calories as unsightly, sluggish white fat.

Daniel B. Mowrey, Ph.D., author of *Fat Management! The Thermogenic Factor*, explains that brown fat is the "organ whose primary job it is to waste excess calories obtained from food that is digested and assimilated, and perhaps already stored away as fat." Note that he includes calories already stored as fat in his list of brown fat's fuel. This means that if you jump-start your brown fat–burning engine, you will not only burn excess calories you will consume in the future, but you will also boost your body's ability to burn already stored white fat!

In any given day, we rarely match up the exact number of calories we consume with the amount we expend. Some days we may consume more calories than we need, and some days we may consume fewer. Most of us in this age of abundance fall into the first category and consume calories in excess of what we need day to day. When this occurs, the body has two avenues from which to choose: to burn the excess through brown fat–activated thermogenesis or to store the caloric surplus as white fat. Unfortunately, many people's brown fat–burning engines are on the blink and do not burn many excess calories. For these individuals, there is a roadblock to fat burning, and the only option left for their bodies is to accumulate white fat.

THERMO—WHAT?

Dr. Mowrey explains that the word *thermogenesis* is taken from the Latin *thermo*, meaning "heat," and *genesis*, meaning "to create." Thermogenesis, therefore, means "the creation of heat, something the human body must do to maintain body temperature at 98.6 degrees F."

While all of us have some degree of thermogenesis at work, people who find it easy to burn excess calories tend to have brown fat that is particularly adept at the thermogenetic process. In people who have brown fat that is underactive or inefficient, the body does not burn fat easily, and they probably have a tendency to store excess calories as white fat. A slim person with an efficiently functioning fat burner can easily convert excess calories into heat energy, while an obese person, even if he or she eats the same number of calories as the slim person, will store the caloric excess as white fat instead.

The ventromedial hypothalamus part of the brain houses our appetite control. Appetite regulation involves a feedback type of mechanism that somehow senses both the insulin and amino acids in the bloodstream. Researchers believe that the ventromedial hypothalamus triggers brown fat tissue activation when an excessive amount of calories is ingested. Obese individuals may have either insufficient brown fat amounts or a faulty triggering of the brown fat they do have.

Researchers in France conducted a study in 1992 that explored the connection between fat storage, thermogenesis, and the metabolic process. The study separated thirty-two women into three different experimental groups. The first were women of average weight without a history of obesity, the second were overweight women who had a history of obesity, and the third group was comprised of women who had just recently been experiencing weight gain and increased difficulty losing weight. The researchers gave each group a dose of pure glucose (sugar water) and measured how the women in each group metabolized the calories.

The results were astounding. The lean women in the first group processed the glucose with an increase in thermogenesis. The overweight women in the second group did not experience an increase in thermogenesis but rather stored the glucose. And the women in the third group, who were not obese but only recently experienced difficulty losing weight, also exhibited a failure in thermogenesis. The researchers concluded that a defect in thermogenesis may actually be a precursor to obesity.

Dr. Mowrey explains that "if the body loses its thermogenic capacity, obesity is certain to occur. It has been estimated that even a 0.1 percent deficit in the number of calories expended through thermogenesis could result in the accumulation of excess fat to the tune of 25 percent of body weight, i.e., obesity."

WHAT <u>NOT</u> TO DO

Okay, you say, so I've got this brown fat surrounding vital organs in my body which, when functioning properly, acts as a superior fat-burning organ. What should I do if I don't burn calories or stored fat easily? How can I jump-start my brown fat–burning engine?

Before I tell you how to increase your body's ability to burn fat, let me tell you what *not* to do: Do not begin a restricted-calorie diet!

No matter how tempting it may be to begin a "quick start"

weight-loss program, I can guarantee you that drastic calorie reduction will ultimately backfire. It will backfire because your body is highly sensitive to caloric deprivation. When you eat far less than the body requires, it senses that food has become scarce and automatically reasons that it must be time to start storing fat for lean times. Rather than continuing to burn calories at its normal rate, the body *slows* its metabolism. The brain, in an attempt to preserve the fat it believes it needs to survive this famine, signals the body to use calories slowly and to burn fat judiciously. Ironically, a restricted-calorie diet only serves to lower metabolism and cause the body to slow its fat-burning potential.

HOW TO START YOUR
FAT-BURNING ENGINE

Brown fat can go a long way in helping you manage the excess calories you may consume on any given day, but it needs to be activated by the right nutrients so that your body will efficiently burn, rather than store, the excess fat you take in.

Gamma linolenic acid (GLA), one of the most potent omega-6 fatty acids found in evening primrose oil, borage oil, and black currant oil, has been found to activate brown fat and boost the metabolic rates in healthy adults. GLA is the raw material needed for certain prostaglandins to ignite the mitochondria's fat-burning process in the body's brown fat.

Interestingly, researchers in Heidelberg, Germany, have found that slimmer adults had a higher proportion of polyunsaturated fatty acids in their blood than did their heavier counterparts. Dr. David Horrobin, a highly respected essential fatty acid researcher, postulates that "fat people may be suffering from a polyunsaturated fatty acid deficiency." Dr. Horrobin has found that GLA is remarkably effective in promoting weight loss, and that evening primrose oil is a particularly valuable dietary component in those who want to lose weight.

In my private practice, I have seen women and men benefit time and time again from the addition of omega fats to their weight-loss plans. Many of my clients who had at least ten pounds or more of weight to lose have reported staggeringly dramatic results with four to eight capsules of 500 mg evening primrose oil. (Of course, after the initial weight-loss period, I always caution my clients that it is biochemically prudent to take an omega-3 source [like flax or fish] along with the omega-6 for optimum balance.)

All too often, dieters on no-fat or low-fat plans will plateau after an initial weight loss. This can be a frustrating time for many dieters, especially when they don't understand why they are not continuing to lose weight at the same pace they were initially. What has occurred is a downshift in the metabolic rate. After a certain period of time on a low-fat, low-calorie diet, the body will recognize the new, lower caloric intake as its sustenance level (it may even think it is starving!) and will slow its metabolism to match the new, lower caloric intake. The hair may become brittle, the nails may crack, and the skin may become dry and flaky, but the body will resist further weight loss. Additional weight loss is stymied because your body now operates at a slower level, a level that may not be healthy but one at which you need fewer calories to subsist.

The only way to activate the metabolism again is to convince the body that it is no longer starving. Along with providing it with adequate protein (which we explored in chapter 5), it is crucial to supply the body with healthy levels of essential fatty acids. My experience and the experience of my colleagues have repeatedly revealed the importance of including the essential fatty acids in a healthy weight-loss plan. Clients who have come to me in confusion and frustration over why they are no longer losing weight and why they are feeling so awful on their diet plans have raved about the rapid improvement they make after we add essential fats and oils to their diets. Energy returns, complexions clear, hair regains its shine, and, remarkably, weight loss resumes! Adding essential fatty acids to the diet is critical for boosting metabolic rate and activating the brown fat–burning engine.

CHAPTER EIGHT

The Omega-3 Oils

How Flax and Fish Oils Improve Health and Boost Metabolism

B EFORE WE EXPLORE the wonderful health benefits of the omega oils, I want to briefly review the basics of fats and oils. For the purpose of the review, I will be using the term *fat* to cover both fats and oils. Fats and oils are actually both *lipids*. Fat is a lipid that is solid at room temperature, while oils are lipids that are liquid at room temperature.

FAT BASICS

Fat is one of the six basic nutrients necessary for sustaining human life; the other five nutrients are protein, carbohydrates, water, vitamins, and minerals. Fats are comprised of three different types of atoms: hydrogen, oxygen, and carbon. These atoms chemically bond to create a fatty acid molecule. Fat can be either saturated or unsaturated, depending on the number of hydrogen atoms it contains and the number of bonds between the carbon atoms.

In saturated fats, carbon atoms are linked together by single bonds and are almost completely paired up with hydrogen atoms. Animal fats as well as coconut oil and palm kernel oil are examples of saturated fats. Because its carbon atoms are packed together with hydrogen atoms, a saturated fat has few gaps in its chemical makeup and tends to be solid at room temperature.

When carbon atoms in fat molecules are connected by double-bonds and not directly paired with hydrogen atoms, the result is an unsaturated fat. Because of the gaps in their chemical makeup, unsaturated fats are more fluid than saturated fats. Unsaturated fats can be monounsaturated or polyunsaturated, depending on the number of double-bonds between their carbon atoms. Monounsaturated fats, such as olive oil, canola oil, or peanut oil have one (*mono* means one) carbon-to-carbon double-bond, while polyunsaturated fats (*poly* means many), such as corn, soy, sesame, and sunflower oils, have two or more double-bonds between carbon atoms.

Polyunsaturated fats also come in two forms: *cis* and *trans* (remember the hazards of transfats I warned you about in chapter 4). Whether a polyunsaturated fat presents in a *cis* or *trans* form depends on which side of the double-carbon bond the hydrogen atoms lie. When both hydrogen atoms are on the same side of the double-carbon bond, the result is a *cis* fat. When the hydrogen atoms are on opposite sides of the carbon bond, the result is a *trans* fat. Transfats are more stable than *cis* fats and less likely to become rancid quickly. That is why food processors love them. Unfortunately, as we now know, they are also more hazardous to your health.

Fatty acids are further categorized by numbering where the carbon bond is located at the end of the fat molecule. Chemists use the "omega" numbering system for this type of categorizing. As we will explore in the next three chapters, knowing the omega number of the type of fat you are consuming can go a long way toward improving your health and enabling you to use fat for optimal physical performance.

ESSENTIAL OMEGAS

Three of the most well-known and well-researched omega fats are the omega-3s, omega-6s, and omega-9s. Omega-3 and omega-6 oils are considered essential fatty acids because the body is unable to manufacture these types of fatty acids on its own. Even though omega-9 oils are not considered essential, they are so rich in health benefits that I strongly recommend including them as well in your daily dietary plan.

Both the omega-3 and omega-6 families of oils are made up of primary essential fatty acids. Alpha linolenic acid (LNA) leads the omega-3 family of oils, while linoleic acid (LA) heads the omega-6 family. In perfect circumstances, our bodies are able to convert alpha linolenic acid in omega-3 oils into eicosapentaenoic acid (EPA) and then into docosahexaenoic acid (DHA). The linoleic acid from omega-6 oils can be converted into gamma linolenic acid (GLA) and arachidonic acid (AA). If our metabolisms are functioning without any undue interference, the EPA and GLA we have made from our consumption of omega oils is then converted into life-essential beneficial prostaglandins. As discussed in earlier chapters, healthy prostaglandin production is critical to the regulation of our entire physical system—from growth and tissue repair to energy production and fat metabolism.

Unfortunately, many factors can inhibit the conversion of alpha linolenic acid and linoleic acid into these life-sustaining elements. Everyday occurrences such as stress, pollution, and aging can interfere with the process, as can nutritional deficiencies, viral infections, diabetes, and alcohol consumption. Amazingly, researchers have recently found that excess sugar consumption and a high intake of transfats can also work to prevent the healthy transformation of omega fats into GLA, DHA, and EPA.

To benefit fully from the omega oils we are going to explore in this and subsequent chapters, it is crucial that you reduce as many of the interfering elements in your life as possible. While no one can halt the aging process, most of us should have little problem cutting back (or eliminating) alcohol, sugar, and transfat consumption. In addition to trying to limit the external interferences to this metabolic process, I strongly believe in the benefits of increasing the intake of direct sources of GLA, DHA, and EPA. By consuming direct sources of these essential nutrients, you can bypass any roadblocks in your metabolic conversion process and avail yourself of the complete benefits that GLA, DHA, and EPA have to offer.

OMEGA-3 OILS

The remainder of this chapter will focus on the omega-3 oils, including their derivatives, EPA and DHA, and their subsequent benefits in improving your complete physical and metabolic health. Discussions of the omega-6 and omega-9 oils follow in chapters 9 and 10.

Alpha linolenic acid (LNA), the primary omega-3 fatty acid, can be found most abundantly in flaxseeds, hemp seeds, pumpkin seeds, walnuts, and dark green leafy vegetables like purslane. Flaxseed oil is the richest source of omega-3 fatty acids.

Flax to the Rescue

Reams of scientific studies have demonstrated how important flax oil is for everyone's overall health—no matter how old we are. Flaxseed oil (from one to four tablespoons a day) has been shown to lower blood cholesterol levels, elevate the HDLs and lower the LDLs, normalize high blood pressure, improve circulatory problems, and relieve depression, fatigue, and allergies, as well as heal skin conditions like eczema, psoriasis, acne, and dry skin. Disorders like diabetes, mental health problems, and accelerated aging have also been immeasurably helped by flaxseed oil supplementation.

Women will be happy to hear that flaxseed is considered a phytoestrogen. There is emerging research that suggests how vital flaxseed is for the prevention of breast cancer, a disease that currently strikes one in eight women. The phytohormone fiber known as lignans in flax (found in the flaxseed particulate of the shell hull) has the ability to normalize estrogen metabolism and remove the excess estrogens thought to fuel breast cancer.

Best of all for weight loss, omega-3 fats found in flax are involved in fat burning because they enable the body's thermostat to be reset, thereby stoking the metabolic fires. If you are not a flax oil lover, then consider supplementation via capsules. One tablespoon of flaxseed oil equals about twelve large capsules.

As mentioned earlier, EPA is an important derivative of LNA and is essential to prostaglandin production. Direct sources of

EPA, which enable you to bypass any metabolic conversion difficulties, include cold-water fish such as salmon, tuna, mackerel, herring, and trout. People who dislike fish or who prefer to ensure their daily intake with supplements will find fish oil capsules of great benefit. DHA, the next major derivative of LNA, is also found in abundance in cold-water fish and fish oil supplements. I regularly recommend one 1,000 mg supplement of Super MaxEPA two to three times daily as an EPA/DHA supplement for my non-fish-eating clients. DHA is also available separately in supplements made from microalgae for vegetarians or those who have difficulty digesting fish oil.

EPA and DHA both have far-reaching physical health benefits as well as mental and emotional health benefits. They are found in the greatest quantities in the brain, eyes, adrenal glands, and male testes.

DHA is the most prevalent fat in the brain and the nervous system, cushioning the neurons and enabling the electrical signals they send to reach their destination clearly. As time goes on, this DHA cushion can erode, and the body is unable to replenish it. Therefore, we need to consume enough dietary omega-3 oils or DHA supplements to keep the brain and nervous system protected. Unfortunately, if you are eating a no- to low-fat diet, there is no way you can take in enough DHA to protect the brain and nervous system.

The primary building block of the brain and the retina of the eye, DHA is critical for the healthy functioning of both organs. As discussed in chapter 1, 60 percent of the brain is comprised of fat. Of that 60 percent, DHA is the most abundant. As the primary structural fatty acid in both the brain and the retina of the eye, DHA is essential for optimal mental and visual functioning.

EPA, the other derivative fatty acid of the omega-3 oils, benefits other parts of the body. EPA was heralded as the essential fatty acid responsible for the low level of cardiovascular disease found in the Eskimo population. Even though Eskimos consume very high levels of saturated fats, they rarely have heart attacks. Studies correlated this low occurrence of cardiovascular disease with the Eskimo's diet, which is rich in cold-water fish. Researchers found that the EPA in the cold-water fish blocked the potentially damaging effects of the saturated fats by preventing blood platelets from clumping together and clogging arteries, which in turn blocks blood flow. In other studies, EPA was found to lower blood cholesterol and improve the ratio of HDL (good) cholesterol to LDL (bad) cholesterol.

EPA has been found to strengthen platelet walls, ensuring against rupture and dangerous clotting. In fact, both omega-3 and omega-6 oils have been found to help stabilize all cell membranes, resulting in more fluid, flexible cells. Better fluidity and flexibility of the cell membranes enhance more effective exchange between membrane layers of the inner and outer cell nutrients. Rebuilding and repairing of tissue is dependent on efficient nutrient exchange. Moreover, since "leaky" or unhealthy cells are at the root of so many modern-day maladies, running the gamut from allergic response to immune system depression, whatever will fortify the cellular membrane walls is absolutely crucial. Both of the omega families strengthen membrane walls on a cellular level.

Today's typical twentieth-century diet contains very few foods which are high in omega-3 fatty acids. Foods that contain omega-3s tend to spoil easily because of the unsaturated oils, which tend to attract oxygen because of the gaps in their chemical makeup. As a result, they become oxidized or rancid more quickly than saturated oils. Yet, at the same time, the unsaturated characteristics of these oils also make them healthful to our bodies. The tendency of unsaturated fats to attract oxygen benefits us tremendously when we consume them. They help carry oxygen through the body via the blood-stream. Unfortunately, as discussed in chapter 4, food manu-facturers often replace unsaturated oils with hydrogenated transfatty oils, which extend the shelf life of a product but also endanger our health.

Boost Your Metabolism with Omega-3s

A diet rich in essential fats and oils works to increase metabolic rate and improve the entire system of energy production. With this increase in metabolism, weight loss is not only possible but inevitable. Blood sugar levels are balanced and food cravings become a thing of the past.

To fully appreciate how the omega fats work to increase metabolism and balance blood sugar levels, let's review insulin resistance and blood glucose levels, as discussed in chapter 3.

The primary role of insulin is to regulate the body's blood sugar or glucose. If the metabolism is working properly, it will regulate glucose levels and keep blood sugar within normal limits. For example, after a meal, glucose levels will rise. In order to bring the blood sugar down to an appropriate level, the pancreas releases insulin. The muscles respond to the insulin and use the excess sugar as energy or store it as glycogen. Remember, muscles are only able to store a small overage of glucose as glycogen. Whatever cannot be stored as glycogen gets stored as fat.

In this way, the pancreas, with the aid of insulin and glucagon, is constantly working to maintain healthy glucose levels in the bloodstream. All too often, however, this system of checks and balances fails to work properly, and a condition called "insulin resistance" develops.

In insulin-resistant individuals, the muscles do not respond to normal levels of insulin, forcing the pancreas to send large amounts of insulin to the muscles so that they can convert excess sugar to energy or glycogen. Research has shown that almost all individuals suffering from obesity, diabetes, and/or high blood pressure are prone to insulin resistance. In fact, many experts now believe that insulin resistance is a precursor to obesity, causing excess body weight to seriously impact the health of the individual.

So, what can we do to combat this all-too-common plague of insulin resistance? How can we safely lose weight and enable our metabolisms to resume their proper, healthy functioning? The answers lie with the omega oils.

Researchers have found that the typical American diet, which is low in omega-3 fatty acids but relatively high in saturated fat and processed refined oils, can often contribute to the development of insulin resistance. Lab animals who were fed a diet high in saturated fats and refined oils, and low in omega-3s, were found to develop insulin resistance. Now here's the amazing part. Adding omega-3 oils to the diets of these lab animals put an end to their insulin resistance! The animals returned to full health with normal metabolisms. Although they continued to consume other types of fats in addition to the omega-3 oils, they remained free of insulin resistance.

This study reveals the absolute necessity of adding to or increasing the level of omega-3 oils in the diets of insulin-resistant Americans. I highly recommend the addition of omega-3 oils (starting with one tablespoon of flaxseed oil daily) to the diets of all individuals who are suffering from obesity, diabetes, and high blood pressure. Omega-3 oils have been clearly demonstrated to help combat the scourge of insulin resistance. They will help restore the healthy functioning of the metabolism in order to burn fat calories for energy rather than storing them as fat.

And there's more! Adding omega-3s to a diet high in saturated fats and refined oils also appears to prevent obesity in lab animals. In a 1996 study in which mice prone to diabetes and obesity were fed high-fat diets, the fattest ones were those fed omega-6 oils or saturated fat; the leanest were those fed omega-3 oils. The study went on to note that the variation in weight between the mice fed the high omega-6 fat diet (primarily soybean oil) and the mice fed the high omega-3 fat diet (primarily fish oil) was comparable to the variation in weight between a 225-pound man and a 150-pound man—*even though both diets were comprised of equal calories and fat percentages*!

This study reveals the amazing benefits of adding omega oils to your diet. Without reducing calories or increasing exercise levels, the lab subjects who were given omega-3 oils were significantly lighter than their counterparts who were fed only saturated fats or omega-6 oils. Omega-3 oils, again, proved to be effective in preventing obesity, even in subjects who were genetically predisposed to obesity. This is wonderful news for anyone struggling with excess weight and a slowed metabolism. The addition of omega-3s into the diet will undoubtedly improve metabolic rate and reduce the tendency toward fat storage.

I want to caution, however, against any inclination to view omega-6 oils as "bad" as a result of the research study cited above. Many omega-6 oils like corn oil are refined and processed or, as in the case of soybean oil, partially hydrogenated. They have therefore lost their fat-burning potential as well as other healthful properties. As we will see in the next chapter, achieving a healthy balance between unprocessed omega-3 and unprocessed omega-6 oils is quickly proving to be the most beneficial plan for healthy metabolic functioning and lasting weight loss.

CHAPTER NINE

The Omega-6 Oils
How GLA-rich Oils Like Evening Primrose Improve Health and Boost Metabolism

OMEGA-6 ESSENTIAL FATTY ACIDS may be derived from both plant and animal sources. Plant sources of omega-6 include unprocessed, unheated vegetable oils, such as corn, safflower, sunflower, soy, cottonseed, and sesame oils. They are also found in abundant supply in certain botanicals such as borage, evening primrose, black currant seeds, and gooseberry oils as well as in raw nuts and seeds, legumes, and leafy greens. Animal sources of omega-6s are primarily lean meats and organ meats, as well as mother's milk.

As stated in the previous chapter, the omega-6 family of essential fatty acids is led by linoleic acid (LA), which is absorbed by the body and then converted into two derivative fatty acids, gamma linolenic acid (GLA) and arachidonic acid (AA). Conjugated linoleic acid (CLA) is somewhat different than the first two. In a perfectly functioning body, the GLA and AA derived from linoleic acid is then converted into two forms of prostaglandins.

PROSTAGLANDIN BASICS

Prostaglandin production is essential to health and well-being. As discussed earlier, prostaglandins are hormonelike substances that control the functioning of most of the body's life-sustaining systems. They control the circulatory system, heart function, the skin (our largest organ), and the immune system. Those who suffer from an inadequate or an imbalanced supply of specific prostaglandins may be vulnerable to heart attacks, high blood pressure, asthma, arthritis, infertility, and/or migraines, and more.

It is important to understand that the body cannot store prostaglandins; it manufactures them from the fatty acids consumed as they are needed. Therefore, sufficient levels of essential fatty acids must be consumed daily to meet the body's prostaglandin requirements.

The various essential fatty acids are converted into different prostaglandins, each of which performs specific roles. In a healthy, functioning body, GLA is eventually converted into a prostaglandin called PGE1, AA is converted into PGE2, and the EPA discussed in the previous chapter is converted into PGE3. Each of these prostaglandins carries out various functions.

PGE1 and PGE3 have been proven to be of value in protecting against coronary disease. Derived from both linoleic and alpha linolenic acids, these two vital prostaglandins protect the functioning of the heart by keeping the blood platelets slippery and free flowing. PGE1 and PGE3 work to prevent blood clotting. PGE2, derived from AA, is inflammatory, appears to trigger platelet aggregation, and actually encourages blood platelets to clot. However, all three prostaglandin forms, PGE1, PGE2, and PGE3, must be present to ensure a properly functioning clotting system. The body needs enough PGE2 to ensure healthy clotting (clotting is, after all, what keeps us from bleeding to death!), yet it must have enough PGE1 and PGE3 to balance the equation and protect against unhealthy overclotting, which can lead to heart attack and stroke. This is a perfect example of the importance of balance in prostaglandin production. A deficiency in any of the prostaglandin forms would throw this delicate balance off-kilter.

Research has taught us that some prostaglandins, like PGE1 and PGE3, are anti-inflammatory, and some, like PGE2, cause inflammation. Likewise, PGE1 appears to function as a diuretic, while PGE2 triggers the kidneys to retain salt and encourages water retention. In these and many other instances, PGE1 and PGE2 serve as a system of checks and balances within the body.

Based on this data, it would certainly be deceptively easy to categorize GLA (and PGE1) as the "good" fatty acid and AA (and its derivative PGE2) as the "bad" one. But it isn't that simple.

Far from being completely harmful all of the time, AA and its derivative PGE2 are necessary for many healthy physical processes. As the second most abundant fatty acid in the brain, AA must be present for healthy brain and synapse functioning. It is only when overproduced or imbalanced that AA and PGE2 can lead to illness and disease. Rather than eliminating AA and its prostaglandin derivatives from the diet, the goal should be to consume AA in a healthy balance with other omega-6s, namely GLA and omega-3 oils.

THE IMPORTANCE OF BALANCE

The body runs into trouble when its food sources are so out of balance that it ends up producing too much of one type of prostaglandin and having little raw material to convert into other prostaglandins. It is clear that the twentieth-century diet creates an imbalance in prostaglandin production. The overemphasis on land-animal meats and the underconsumption of cold-water fish and unprocessed oils have left us with an abundance of inflammation-producing prostaglandins (PGE2s) and a scarcity of anti-inflammatory agents (PGE1s).

Inflammatory diseases are rampant in our modern-day society. Many disorders, such as eczema, psoriasis, seborrhea, arthritis, asthma, and a whole host of allergies, are inflammatory processes that are widespread in the United States. Most of these disorders are treated with medication and topical ointments that address the symptoms but not the cause of the problem. I have recommended GLA for years to my patients who are suffering from skin disorders, such as eczema and psoriasis, and have witnessed firsthand the remarkable healing that occurs.

Years of experience have taught me that the anti-inflammatory properties of GLA and PGE1 are wonderful healing agents. GLA helps combat allergy symptoms and the muddle-headed feeling that often accompanies them. In fact, this muddle-headed feeling is actually the result of brain inflammation, which is also ameliorated by GLA supplements.

Dr. David Horrobin of the Institute for Innovative Medicine in Montreal addressed the importance of GLA and its prostaglandin derivative when stating that "the level of PGE1 is of crucial importance to the body. A fall in the level of PGE1 will lead to a potentially catastrophic series of untoward consequences including increased vascular reactivity, enhanced [blood clotting], elevated cholesterol production, enhanced risk of autoimmune disease, enhanced release of AA, enhanced risk of inflammatory disorders, and susceptibility to depression."

DIETARY AND SUPPLEMENTAL SOURCES

Even if your diet consists of foods with a high content of corn, safflower, or soybean oils, you may not be consuming healthy amounts of omega-6s. In order to convert these oils into GLA, they must be *unheated*, *unprocessed*, and in the *cis* form. Hydrogenated transfats will not do the job!

In a healthy metabolism, *cis* linoleic acid is easily converted into GLA. Found in unheated, unprocessed vegetable oils like corn, soybean, safflower, and sunflower oils, *cis* linoleic acid is necessary for GLA production. However, the process of conversion from *cis* linoleic acid to GLA can be thwarted in many ways. For example, if *cis* linoleic acid is heated, as are most of the oils we consume every day, some of the *cis* linoleic acid is converted into *trans* linoleic acid. Transfats cannot be converted into GLA and actually inhibit the conversion of the remaining *cis* linoleic acid into GLA.

Even if we do manage to consume adequate amounts of *cis* linoleic acid, other factors such as stress, alcohol consumption, and prescription medication can all interfere with the process of conversion into GLA. Because so many factors can be disruptive,

I strongly recommend preformed sources of GLA as a way to circumvent these disruptions. Two of the most potent forms of preformed GLA are evening primrose oil and borage.

As a direct source of preformed GLA, evening primrose oil has been found beneficial in a whole host of physical ailments—from heart attack prevention (due to its anticoagulant properties) to the stimulation of the immune system and cancer prevention. It has been effective in the treatment of a wide range of conditions, including splitting or brittle nails, lackluster hair, asthma, and hangover. Substance abuse recovery programs often use evening primrose oil as a nutritional therapy for drug cravings.

With regard to women's health, evening primrose oil offers a broad array of benefits. In study after study, women have found it to be outstanding for the treatment of irritability, mood changes, headaches, anxiety, premenstrual syndrome, and perimenopausal discomforts such as fluid retention and breast tenderness. My clients swear it is the only natural therapy that relieves their migraine headaches. Plus, many menopausal readers have told me that four to six 500 mg evening primrose capsules per day have stopped their hot flashes and night sweats.

GLA in the form of evening primrose oil has also been found to be remarkably effective in another all-too-common immune system disorder, rheumatoid arthritis. This debilitating illness results when the body's immune system begins to function improperly and attacks its own joints and surrounding membranes. Inflammation results from this attack and causes severe pain for the sufferer. Again, the inflammation in this case is connected to an oversupply of AA and its derivative,

PGE2. If sufficient quantities of GLA and PGE1 are not available to counteract the PGE2, the inflammation will progress unchecked. However, studies have shown that with the addition of GLA and PGE1, many sufferers of rheumatoid arthritis have reported an easing of painful joint inflammation. Once the GLA and PGE1 have an opportunity to balance out the excess AA and PGE2 (which may take several months in some cases), the body is able to restore itself with a healthy balance of prostaglandins.

WEIGHT LOSS AND GLA

In addition to fighting coronary heart disease, arthritis, asthma, and cancer, GLA can also promote weight loss. To understand how GLA increases the body's fat-burning ability, refer back to chapter 7, where we explored the amazing properties of brown fat. Brown fat, you will remember, helps burn excess calories. If the body's brown fat is dormant or inactive, excess calories are stored as fat. If the brown fat is active and functioning, the excess calories are burned as heat.

GLA has been found to activate dormant brown fat, enabling the body to turn on its fat-burning engine. The prostaglandins formed by GLA accelerate the mitochondria in the brown fat, which works to burn calories. As discussed in chapter 7, a study showed that evening primrose oil supplements resulted in a weight loss of over 10 percent by individuals who had participated in the study. The weight loss was achieved *without* dieting and *without* the subjects reporting any feelings of deprivation or hunger. GLA, abundant in both borage and evening prim-rose oil, acts as the key that turns on the body's brown fat–burning engine.

I have counseled many individuals who have experienced the weight-loss benefits of GLA. In one case, I was working with two women, both models, who were trying to lose those stubborn last five pounds. The women had been dieting and exercising for months, to no avail. Nothing they did enabled them to shed those last excess pounds until I had them each add two tablespoons of unheated, unprocessed safflower oil— one of the best sources of *cis* linoleic acid available—to their daily diets. Within three weeks, both women reported remark-able results. They both had lost their excess weight without any extra food restriction. Their hair, skin, and nails looked health-ier than they had in years, and they both felt more energetic as a result of the slight increase in fat calories. The *cis* linoleic acid in those two tablespoons of unprocessed safflower oil, which transformed into GLA in their systems, made all the difference.

I have seen the benefits of adding small amounts of GLA into the diet over and over again. In addition to weight loss, as stated earlier, GLA can dramatically relieve many female-related problems, including the symptoms of PMS with its associated bloating, depression, irritability, and cramps. Early in my career, I was working with a woman who was having great difficulty with PMS. I recommended GLA to ease her suf-fering, and she returned with wonderful news. The GLA had eased her premenstrual suffering and she had begun to lose weight again after years of unsuccessful dieting.

CONJUGATED LINOLEIC ACID

Another recently discovered form of linoleic acid that has been in the weight-loss news recently is a compound called conjugated linoleic acid (CLA). According to a recent article by Dallas Clouatre, Ph.D., "adding CLA to the diet for four to eight weeks has been shown to substantially reduce the amount of fat in the body (4.34 percent versus 10.13 percent in one study) and to moderately increase the amount of lean tissue."

Once abundant in dairy and beef products, CLA is traditionally produced in the meat and milk of grazing farm animals such as sheep and cattle. However, the key to the production of CLA appears to be in the grass feed of these animals. Unfortunately, today's cattle are fed an amalgam of chemically altered grain-based feeds rather than their traditional grass feed. This has left CLA in short supply in its once natural sources.

Thankfully, CLA is available in supplement form and can be found in most health-food stores. Researchers first discovered the benefits of CLA when investigating its cancer-fighting properties. It has been proven to support tissue growth and prevent the loss of muscle mass that often accompanies advancing cancers. As an important antioxidant, it can protect and strengthen the immune system to help ward off potential invaders. Moreover, CLA has also been found to have positive effects on serum cholesterol levels. Research subjects treated with healthy doses of CLA experienced a reduction of harmful LDL levels without a reduction in healthy HDL levels.

My years of research and clinical practice have taught me

many things. One of the truths of which I am certain is that unprocessed and unrefined omega-6 oils, including preformed GLA and CLA, are miraculous essential fatty acids that should be added to your diet today if you are interested in losing weight, boosting your immune system, easing allergies, healing skin conditions, or improving your coronary health.

CHAPTER TEN

The Omega-9 Oils

How Olive Oil, Avocados, and Nuts Improve Health and Promote Satiety

UNLIKE THE OMEGA-3 AND OMEGA-6 fatty acids, the omega-9 family of fatty acids are not considered essential fatty acids. However, the health benefits of the omega-9 oils are so extensive that I would consider myself negligent if I did not include a chapter extolling their virtues.

The omega-9 family of oils is led by the monounsaturated fatty acid known as oleic acid. While olive oil is one of the best sources of oleic acid, it also may be found in avocados and a large variety of nuts (peanuts, almonds, pistachios, pecans, cashews, hazelnuts, and macadamias).

As monounsaturates, the omega-9 oils are fatty acids that have a single double-bond between their carbon atoms. Because of this one double-bond, monounsaturated oils are somewhat more stable than their polyunsaturated counterparts. This means that monounsaturated oils are less prone to oxidation and are able to resist rancidity at higher temperatures than polyunsaturates.

Monounsaturated oils have been shown to have wonderful health benefits when consumed as part of a balanced diet. Research at the University of Texas Health Science Center directed by Dr. Scott Grundy has focused on the coronary health benefits of monounsaturated oils. In the March 1986 *New England Journal of Medicine*, Dr. Grundy reported that the monounsaturated type of fatty acid (oleic acid) found in olive oil was more successful at protecting arteries from cholesterol buildup than the low-fat, high-carbohydrate diets prescribed by so many physicians. Again we see how low-fat, high-carbohydrate diets, often touted as a cure-all for many of the nation's ills, are actually outperformed by diets rich in heart-healthy omega oils.

Monounsaturated oils are critical for more than heart health. A recent study by Dr. Alicja Wolk, in Stockholm, Sweden, reported that monounsaturated fats can help reduce a woman's risk for breast cancer. The women in Dr. Wolk's study with the highest risk of breast cancer had the lowest intake of monounsaturated fats. Conversely, the women with the lowest risk for breast cancer had the highest intake of monounsaturated fats. "It is a question of replacing one fat with another," said Dr. Wolk. Adding monounsaturated fats to a diet already laden with transfats and saturated fats will result in an overload of fat calories. Instead, replace the transfats and saturated fats with healthy omega-3, -6, and -9 oils. While cautioning against drawing too many causal connections from Dr. Wolk's study, Dr. Walter Willett of the Harvard School of Public Health concurs that monounsaturated oils should be used whenever possible in place of saturated fats and transfats.

The oleic acid in monounsaturated omega-9 oils also acts to boost the effect of omega-3 fatty acids in the blood. By enhancing the incorporation of omega-3s into the cells of the body, monounsaturated oleic acid strengthens cell functioning and allows for greater fluidity of the cell structure.

OLIVE OIL

As we have discussed in earlier chapters, the people of the Mediterranean region have been enjoying the benefits of a diet rich in omega-9 monounsaturated fatty acids for countless generations. Known throughout medical research for their low incidence of coronary disease, Mediterranean people liberally employ olive oil for all their cooking needs. However, it is important to consider how the traditional Mediterranean production of olive oil differs from commercial oil production in the United States.

Olive oil produced in the Mediterranean countries of Italy, Spain, Greece, France, Portugal, Tunisia, and Morocco is graded into three categories during the production process. These three grades are extra-virgin, virgin, and pure. The first two grades, extra-virgin and virgin, are cold-pressed oils, which means that no heat is employed in their production process. Cold-pressed oils are extracted by hand or with hydraulic presses which use no heat to squeeze out the oils. Extra-virgin olive oil is made with the finest olives from the first pressing. Virgin oil, the next grade, is also made from the first pressing but uses a lesser quality olive than the first. And "pure" olive oil, while it sounds healthy, is actually a combination of refined (usually heat-processed) oils from later pressings. Remember that heat can quickly turn natural, healthy oils into hazardous transfats.

OIL PRODUCTION TODAY

To fully appreciate the importance of cold-pressed oils, it is important to understand the history of oil production in America and how it has changed in the last century. From the discovery of oil extraction up until about 100 years ago, all oil was cold pressed. Extracting oils from nuts, seeds, and fruits was a critical task, and every village had its own oil vendor. It was the responsibility of the oil vendor to use whatever means necessary to extract oil from the local produce (be it olives, flaxseeds, or another oil-rich food source). Then the oil vendor, much like all the other produce vendors of that time, would sell his fresh oil door to door. The oil of that time was cold-pressed and unaltered by yet-to-be-discovered preservatives. It was treated as a perishable, often expensive commodity, and handled with care. The people of that era knew that their oil could become rancid if exposed to heat or light, so they transferred their precious oil into earthenware containers and stored it in a cool, dark place.

This was a time when food was either fresh or rancid. There were no chemical preservatives. While salt was used to cure meats and it was possible to can fruits and vegetables, most food was consumed hours, not weeks, after it was first prepared.

And it's even worse with oils. Today we don't even question whether the oil we are buying is "fresh." Most Americans aren't aware that oil was once a highly perishable product that quickly became rancid if exposed to heat or light. All we know about oil is the row upon row of clear, plastic bottles that sit for weeks or even months in our supermarkets.

At the turn of the century, when the Industrial Revolution was in full swing, engineers developed a process of quickly and efficiently extracting oil that could be stored for weeks without turning rancid. As was the case for many of the innovations of the Industrial Revolution, this new process was far less labor intensive and far more cost effective than the agrarian method of oil extraction. However, as was also the case for many of the innovations of that time, this process had a downside that was not fully appreciated until many decades later.

The engineers of the Industrial Revolution developed very sophisticated chemical refining processes that removed or destroyed nearly all the life-sustaining nutrients present in oils so they could sit almost indefinitely without decaying. But, these clever refining methods also created many poisonous compounds like transfatty acids, free radicals, and other toxic substances. And that is what we are left with today on our supermarket shelves—ultra-refined, heat-processed oils that have been stripped of the essential nutrients that provide critical health benefits. Most of the oils on our grocery shelves are produced by the same few giant corporations that produce most of the oil in the United States. The heat processing they employ creates transfats and free radicals that prey on healthy cells.

There are a multitude of processing methods that commercial oil producers employ to render our oil suitable for long stays on a market shelf. They include deodorization, bleaching, and alkali refining. These processes remove virtually all the vitamin E, lecithin, and beta carotene from the oil. Worse yet, refining oil destroys much of the omega-3 and omega-6 essential fatty acids, converting them into poisonous transfats. It is clear that wisely choosing the oil you use can go a long way toward helping you reap the benefits of healthy, unrefined oils. I recommend buying extra-virgin olive oil stored in an opaque container whenever possible.

Canola oil is second only to olive oil in its percentage of monounsaturated fat and is a source of the healthy omega-3s as well. It can be used in no-heat recipes and is a versatile cooking oil because it is practically flavorless. Derived from rapeseed, canola is also the oil lowest in saturated fat. If a high-quality olive oil is too expensive for your budget, you can create an oil for yourself which is half olive oil and half canola oil. Some people actually prefer the lighter taste of this 50/50 combination. Try to purchase oils that have been cold pressed (not heat refined) and stored in an opaque (not clear) container. Never purchase oil in quantities greater than you will use in a month's time, and be sure to store your oil in a cool, dark place.

AVOCADOS AND NUTS

Omega-9 fatty acids may also be found in other food sources such as avocados and nuts. With their reputations much maligned during the low-fat craze, avocados and nuts are now enjoying a resurgence in popularity due to the recent media focus on healthy fats.

Avocados were once thought to be as dangerous for the heart and waistline as transfat-filled French fries or potato chips. Now, researchers understand the importance of monounsaturated vegetable fats in a healthy dietary program. Like all healthy fats, avocados are a calorie- and nutrient-dense food source, and a little goes a long way. A relatively small quantity of avocado (sliced or mashed into guacamole) offers a substantial satiety response. This means that the omega-9 fat in avocado (and in olive oil and many types of nuts) will allow you to feel satisfied and full for a long time after you've eaten. This satiety factor plays an important role in preventing unhealthy binges on transfat- and sugar-laden snack foods.

Many different types of nuts, including peanuts, almonds, pistachios, pecans, cashews, hazelnuts, and macadamias are also a wonderful source of omega-9 monounsaturated fatty acids. As with avocados, nuts are a calorie- and nutrient-dense food that provides hours of satiety after eating. Nuts are also chockfull of important minerals which many Americans are lacking, including potassium, zinc, and magnesium. Almonds, cashews, and pecans are excellent sources of potassium. Magnesium may be found in almonds and cashews. And zinc is most abundant in pecans, as well as in almonds, hazelnuts, and peanuts.

In a now-famous study, over 26,000 Seventh-Day Adventists who consumed nuts at least five times a week were found to have had a 50 percent lower heart attack risk than the members of the study who rarely ate nuts. The study credited the monounsaturated fat in the nuts as being the critical factor in reducing coronary heart disease.

I hope I have made it clear that the omega-9 family of monounsaturated oils, while not technically "essential fatty acids," should be an essential part of your balanced diet. From fighting the buildup of cholesterol deposits in the blood to warding off the evils of breast cancer, monounsaturated oils play a critical role in protecting health. For those among us who are struggling with extra weight, the monounsaturated omega-9s play an important role in creating a significant satiety response. By allowing us to feel full and satisfied for hours after eating, foods rich in omega-9s help us guard against binges on unhealthy sugars and transfats.

CHAPTER ELEVEN

Omega Remedies for Overall Health

A MERICANS SUFFER FROM a host of illnesses resulting from dietary imbalances. From allergies and skin disorders to rheumatoid arthritis and depression, many struggle endlessly to ease the symptoms of diseases that they may unwittingly be creating themselves.

Today, the average American diet is laden with meats, highly processed carbohydrates, and sugars that trigger an overabundance of inflammation-producing prostaglandins. Because comparatively little cold-water fish and unprocessed oils are consumed, there is no way to balance inflammation-producing prostaglandins with EPA and GLA, the anti-inflammatory agents derived from them. Thus, many people are left struggling to manage an overload of inflammatory agents in the body.

As we discussed in chapter 9, chronic inflammation is one sign of a malfunctioning immune system. Inflammation is usually the result of an army of white blood cells coming in to attack an invader. When the invader is conquered, the immune system recognizes its work as done, and the inflammation subsides. With chronic inflammation, the immune army continues to attack long after any invader is threatening. Many of today's more prevalent disorders, such as eczema, psoriasis, seborrhea, arthritis, asthma, and a whole host of allergies, are the result of chronic inflammation.

THE DANGERS OF SUGAR

Along with this overproduction of inflammation-producing prostaglandins, our high-sugar, highly processed carbohydrate diets make matters even worse. In my 1996 book, *Get the Sugar Out*, I explain how overconsuming sugar and processed carbohydrates leaves us vulnerable to illness and disease. Simple sugars and processed carbohydrates are known immunosuppressants that paralyze the immune system in a variety of ways. They

- destroy the germ-killing powers of white blood cells for as long as five hours after ingestion.
- lessen the production of antibodies, which track down foreign invaders in the bloodstream.
- interfere with the transport of vitamin C, one of the body's most important nutrients and antioxidants.
- weaken the immune system by causing mineral imbalances and sometimes allergic reactions.
- make cells more permeable and therefore vulnerable to invaders by neutralizing the action of the essential fatty acids.

OMEGAS AND THE IMMUNE SYSTEM

A well-functioning immune system is the body's best defense against any foreign invader—from a simple cold to cancer. Nothing plays as crucial a role in good health as a powerful immune system. With proper care and nourishment, the immune system gives lifelong protection from all types of illnesses.

The immune system is a well-coordinated army of specialized organs, tissues, and chemicals that identify and eliminate foreign invaders. Comprised of lymph nodes, spleen, bone marrow, thymus gland, tonsils, and lymphocytes (white blood cells), this system circulates twenty trillion immune cell warriors throughout the body to seek out and destroy invasive bacteria, viruses, yeasts, and cancer cells.

While genetics certainly factor into the strength and resilience of the immune system, current research has shown that critical vitamins, minerals, and food compounds can also boost the immune system. A diet containing protective nutrients can strongly influence the performance of the white blood cells, the front-line warriors against infection and cancer.

When food, alcohol, and/or stressful life situations leave the immune system compromised, people are much more vulnerable to illness and disease. Every day many of us engage in activities that tax the immune system. We don't get enough sleep, we don't eat nutritionally balanced meals, and we spread ourselves far too thin trying to meet the demands of career, family, and friends. We are overworked, overtired, and overstressed. All of this has a significant impact on health. Researchers have found that stress lowers resistance to viral infections and nearly doubles the chances of catching a cold.

Autoimmune Disorders

Besides taxing the immune system, often beyond capacity, the average American diet can also trigger debilitating autoimmune disorders, which develop when the critical line of immune defense breaks down and, in a sense, gets its attack orders confused. Some researchers attribute autoimmune disorders to an overactive immune system. Rather than simply attacking enemy germs, such as a cold germ or a virus, an overactive immune system begins attacking its own life-supporting organs. Many modern-day diseases, including lupus, rheumatoid arthritis, Crohn's disease, allergies, asthma, diabetes, atherosclerosis, multiple sclerosis, and Parkinson's disease are the result of autoimmune disorders.

According to Donald Rudin, M.D., coauthor of the 1996 book *Omega-3 Oils*, "Normally the immune system is kept under control by the body's essential fatty acid–based regulatory system. But dietary distortions, especially a shortage of the omega-3 fatty acids, are now known to contribute to—or even prompt—the breakdown of the immune system." The key to realigning these disease-producing distortions in the immune system is *balance*. Our modern-day diets are too overloaded with unhealthy transfats and commercially processed omega-6 oils. Regaining healthy immune functioning lies in rebalancing the intake of unprocessed, unheated omega-3 and omega-6 oils and thereby rebalancing the prostaglandin derivatives of these essential oils in the body.

Dr. Rudin goes on to note that he, too, is "convinced that the way to reduce immune disorders is to bring the intake of omega-3 and omega-6 fatty acids into balance, mainly by increasing omega-3 intake to counteract excessive omega-6 intake." While I wholeheartedly agree with Dr. Rudin's prescription for balance, I want to clarify that I believe the "excessive omega-6" intake he refers to is largely an intake of heated, processed oils that are unable to be transformed by the body into valuable GLA and its PGE1 derivative.

Creating a balance of omega-3 and omega-6 essential oils in a dietary plan has resulted in remarkable results in study after study. In several research reports, adding omega-3 oils to the diet had a markedly positive effect on reducing the symptoms and occurrences of inflammatory diseases such as Crohn's disease, rheumatoid arthritis, and a whole host of allergies.

Adding omega-3s (especially flaxseed oil) to a typical modern diet has been found to greatly improve symptoms of autoimmune disorders. Omega-3 fatty acids can block inflammation by sending a message to your genes to slow down production of an important signaling protein called interleukin-1, or IL-1. IL-1 is involved in a great number of diseases, including allergies, Alzheimer's disease, ulcerative colitis, Crohn's disease, atherosclerosis, AIDS, chronic obstructive pulmonary disease, psoriasis, Type 1 diabetes, asthma, multiple sclerosis, and rheumatoid arthritis. Supplementing your diet with omega-3 fatty acids can lower IL-1 levels by as much as 50 percent, a degree of suppression similar to that caused by some steroid drugs.

On the other hand, lowering the amount of omega-3s in a population's diet and increasing omega-6s (which are most likely refined, processed, or even partially hydrogenated) appears to encourage the development of allergies and other inflammation-based diseases. Dr. Rudin reports that Japanese scientist Harumi

Okuyama discovered that there has been a significant increase in the rate of allergies among Japanese babies. Fully one-third of Japanese infants are now diagnosed with allergic conditions. Okuyama correlates this increase to ". . . Westernized changes in the Japanese diet." He says that reduced omega-3 intake, coupled with excessive omega-6 intake, leads to overproduction of irritating omega-6 prostaglandins.

In research study after research study, the importance of achieving a balance of omega-3 and omega-6 oils has been reinforced. We know that excessive amounts of commercially processed omega-6s can promote inflammation, water retention, and blood clotting. We also know that in many people, intake of these refined omega-6s and omega-3s is way out of balance, causing the AA prostaglandin derivatives to flourish while the GLA and EPA derivatives are in short supply. Boosting intake of omega-3 essential fatty acids and adding preformed GLA supplements to the diet increase PGE1 and PGE3 levels and balance excessive PGE2 prostaglandins.

EASING BEHAVIORAL, NEUROLOGICAL, AND PSYCHOLOGICAL DISORDERS WITH OMEGA OILS

In addition to alleviating a multitude of immune disorders, the omega oils have also been found to ease a wide range of behavioral, neurological, and psychological disorders. Attention deficit hyperactive disorder (ADHD), depression, and schizophrenia have all been linked in studies to low brain chemistry levels of essential fatty acids, especially DHA (found in the omega-3 family of fatty acids). Supplementing the diets of research participants with the omega-3 oils, especially flaxseed oil, has been shown to improve symptoms of both specific mental illnesses and ADHD.

In April 1997, the Cornell Medical Center in New York City presented a symposium entitled "Keeping Your Brain in Shape: New Insights into DHA." Research presented at the conference confirmed that supplementing a typical twentieth-century diet with the omega-3 derivative DHA eased a multitude of neurological and psychological symptoms in study participants. Individuals struggling with ADHD, Alzheimer's disease, multiple sclerosis, and schizophrenia reported a reduction of symptoms when DHA was added to their regimen. Researchers at the symposium also reported that DHA supplementation was correlated to lower levels of aggression in criminals and was found to improve neurological development in infants.

Researchers and nutritionists now know that DHA and other fatty acids are essential to the development of the infant brain. In the January 1998 edition of *Pediatrics*, L. John Horwood, M. Sc., B.A., and David M. Fergusson, Ph.D., reported the results of their study, which tracked over 1,000 newborns from birth to eighteen years. As part of their findings, Horwood and Fergusson reported that "the weight of evidence clearly favors the view that exposure to breastfeeding is associated with . . . increases in childhood cognitive ability and educational achievement, with it being likely that these increases reflect the effects of long-chain polyunsaturated DHA, on early neurodevelopment." I have supported the importance of breast-feeding infants for decades and am a great believer in the necessity of adding DHA to infant formulas. While the World Health Organization has acknowledged that DHA is crucial for infant brain development and foreign companies have begun adding these omega oils to their infant formulas, the United States has not yet approved the addition of DHA to infant formulas marketed in this country.

In their book *The Brain Wellness Plan*, neurologist Jay Lombard and nutritionist Carl Germano note how DHA plays a major role in the communication between brain synapses. They describe how DHA can impact the fluidity of brain cell membranes and influence how easily the chemical messages between synapses are relayed. They add that "many researchers believe that changes in the composition and metabolism of fatty acids like DHA may contribute to Alzheimer's. In one major Swedish study, investigators demonstrated that the brain DHA content of Alzheimer's patients was significantly less than the levels in the brains of control patients." My research has shown that in addition to Alzheimer's disease, depression, memory loss, and ADHD may all be linked to low levels of DHA in the brain.

In reviewing the current research on diet and depression, Dr. Simopoulos cites studies that follow rates of depression in the United States and Japan. Researchers have found high levels of omega-3 fatty acid consumption in Japanese fishing villages and among the elderly population who consume a traditional fish-based diet. In these populations, the levels of depression were far below their counterparts in the United States. Simopoulos notes that "the traditional Japanese diet contains about fifteen times more omega-3 fatty acids than the American diet. Careful studies show that the Japanese people have one-tenth the rate of depression of Americans. The difference is even more pronounced between members of the older generations. Approximately 33 percent of the American elderly have symptoms of depression, compared with only 2 percent of the Japanese elderly."

Two researchers from the National Institutes of Health, Joseph Hibbeln and Norman Salem, have begun lengthy investigations into the question of whether and how omega-3 oils relieve depression. Simopoulos notes that "Hibbeln and Salem suggest that the epidemic of depression in the United States might be linked to our increasingly unbalanced diet." Again, the idea of balance arises, stressing the importance of including more omega-3 essential fatty acids in the diet and ensuring that omega-6 consumption contains primarily unprocessed, unheated *cis*-form oils.

Dr. Rudin also conducted many small studies on the interaction between omega oils and mental illness. Rudin notes that in a study of forty-four persons who took part in a pilot study focusing on omega therapy, twelve were mentally ill. Rudin explains that these twelve mentally ill patients also had physical symptoms which suggested an omega-3 deficiency (including dry skin, arthritis, food allergies, headache, and fatigue). He reports that "the improvement in seven of these patients' mental illnesses—agoraphobia, mood disorders, and schizophrenia—mirrored unmistakable improvements in their physical condition, and was a direct response to increased levels of omega-3s in their bodies."

Dr. Rudin presents many case histories that provide compelling evidence to support his assertions in his book, *Omega-3 Oils*. He notes that "in at least seven out of twelve patients, omega-3 fatty acids produced improved behavior, contributed to feelings of well-being, and reduced psychotic thinking. Also, a great many of the mentally ill patients also experienced a lessening of their physical problems—irritable bowel syndrome, joint diseases, tinnitus, food allergies. Thus, there are many possible benefits from omega oil supplementation, including greater peace of mind."

CONCLUSION

I hope it has become clear through the course of this book that all fats are not bad fats and that, in fact, one's body requires certain essential omega fats in order to achieve full health and well-being. If I have succeeded at my task, you are now aware of the importance of the omega oils in a daily dietary plan. You also realize that it is not only possible to lose weight with the omega fats and oils, it is the only way to activate the body's brown fat–burning engine and to boost metabolism along with regular exercise. In the final chapter, I have detailed sample (and simple!) meal plans for breakfast, lunch, and dinner to assist you as you begin to work toward your weight and dietary goals. Remember, simple sugars, processed carbohydrates, and high-glycemic complex carbohydrates only serve to increase fat storage and send the body system into dangerous imbalance. A wide variety of protein, fruits, vegetables, and low-glycemic carbohydrates is necessary. And omega fats are essential—for attaining weight-loss goals, cardiovascular health, enhanced immunity, and clear and calming thought processes.

CHAPTER TWELVE

The Eat Fat, Lose Weight Eating Plan

N O TIME TO COOK and you don't want to rely on fast foods? Well, relax. You can put together the following menu plans in a matter of minutes—as long as your pantry is well stocked with the right ingredients. If you don't have a particular ingredient in the meal plan or don't like a recommended fruit or vegetable, take a peek at the Savvy Substitutes later in the chapter to find out which foods listed in the same category can be traded off for one another (1 cup berries equals ½ grapefruit, for example).

On those occasions when you simply can't get it together, there are even some health choices out there in the fast-food lane. Let's face it—convenience foods are here to stay. Thus, I have included a fast-food meal within the suggested menus for both lunch and dinner.

As you peruse the seven breakfasts, lunches, and dinners I have included, you will notice that many of these meals can be taken with you to work or can be ordered in a restaurant if you, like so many of us these days, frequently go out to eat. What sets these menus apart from so many other "diet" plans is the presence of some kind of fat (olive oil, flaxseed oil, nuts) at almost every meal. This is deliberate. That little bit of fat gives your meal staying power.

As I have emphasized throughout this book, fat is your friend, not your enemy, when it comes to weight loss. Quality fats provide the satiety factor that allows you to feel filled up and satisfied for hours. This makes long-term weight control a breeze and guarantees that you will not feel deprived. Healthy fats stabilize blood sugar levels to keep you from running to the fridge every five minutes.

Here are eleven illuminating tips to help you stop dieting forever:

1. **Don't skip breakfast.** Studies show that breakfast skippers have problems concentrating and lack sustainable energy. You'll be forever searching for coffee, sweets, and soda to give your blood sugar an immediate lift, but soon after you feel drained again and on the prowl for another sugar hit. Just drop a couple of tablespoons of natural peanut or almond butter on some whole-grain crackers as you fly out the door and take an orange to eat at the office. The combo of fat, protein, and carbohydrates will keep you going for up to four hours.

2. **Eat all the colors of the rainbow.** You should get all the protective phytochemicals in various vegetables and fruits. Include a selection of dark, leafy greens (kale and romaine lettuce) and brightly colored vegetables and fruits (tomatoes, sweet potatoes, oranges, and blueberries) to complement your daily variety of protein foods (eggs, organic poultry, lean beef, fish, legumes, and tofu) and healthy fats (olive oil, flaxseed oil, and nuts).

3. Don't eat the same foods every day. Variety is the spice of life, and the more kinds of foods you eat, the greater your chances of taking in all the important nutrients, antioxidants, and phytochemicals that fight diseases like cancer and heart disease. Strive for at least ten different kinds of foods a day instead of just a few.

4. Avoid large portions of pasta and cut down on bread, bagels, and white rice. These processed and fast-acting carbohydrates can put on weight, slow you down, and make you feel like you have a hangover. Consider instead whole-food side dishes of brown rice, yams, or a small baked potato with the skin on. By the way, alcoholic beverages should be viewed as carbohydrates or starches. If you want to indulge once in a while, then cut back on the starches you consume at the same meal. Four ounces of wine is equivalent to about six ounces of beer or one ounce of the hard stuff. If you are going to have a drink, then have it with a high-protein food or appetizer, not by itself.

5. Eat a large lunch and a small dinner. Our caloric and metabolic needs peak at midday. Work with your metabolism, not against it.

6. Use pure water as the beverage of choice. Water decreases hunger and keeps the brain alert. Exercisers and other active people are not the only ones constantly losing water. For example, those who work in dry and overheated offices or who are exposed to air conditioning every day lose almost ten glasses of water per day. So the eight-glasses-of-water-per-day rule is just a bare minimum. For optimum health, strive for at least twelve 8-ounce glasses spread throughout the day. Herbal teas, green tea, and a cup or two of decaffeinated coffee are fine with meals, but these beverages don't count as part of a daily ration of H_2O.

7. **Try not to go more than four hours without eating.** Keeping blood sugar levels steady translates into more weight loss for you.

8. **Snack in the midafternoon.** Learn to grab a handful of almonds, pumpkin seeds, cashews, or an ounce of low-fat cheese with a piece of fruit (like a nice crunchy Granny Smith apple) as a midafternoon snack.

9. **Don't desert dessert.** In other words, don't deprive yourself. A little bit of natural fruit sorbet or even fresh fruit (fresh pineapple is so good for your digestion) will give your sweet tooth just the satisfaction it needs. Or perhaps a couple (just a couple now) of dried figs, dates, or apricots with some nuts or a tablespoon of nut butter made from almonds, cashews, or sesame seeds (tahini) when you have that hankering for something sweet. The fat and protein in the nut butters will keep your appetite in check and prevent you from going overboard on the dried fruit. If you're out and about and dying for a quick lift, then pop into your local health-food store or supermarket for a Balance Bar, which should keep you going another two to three hours with its healthy ratio of protein, carbs, and fats.

10. **When you go out to eat, tell the waiter to please remove the bread.** Instead, order a seafood cocktail or grilled portobello mushroom to get you started and take the edge off your hunger. In this way you won't be tempted to fill up on carbs. See what you can order to substitute for the potatoes, pasta,

and rice that usually accompany the main course. I always ask for more veggies or another salad.

11. Ensure proper dietary intake. To guarantee the intake of all vitamins, minerals, and essential fatty acids, consider the following dietary supplements especially if you are not a fish eater, skip meals, and/or eat out frequently.

Supplement	Recommended Dosage
Super MaxEPA	1,000 mg 2 to 3 times daily with meals
Flaxseed oil	1 tablespoon or 12 capsules daily
GLA	90 mg 2 times daily with meals
Female multiple	2 with breakfast, lunch, and dinner
Male multiple	1 with breakfast, lunch, and dinner
Weight-loss formula (fat-burning minerals, herbs, enzymes, and amino acids)	2 twice daily with meals

If you are not able to find these supplements at your health-food store, call UniKey at 1-800-888-4353.

THE HEALTHY PANTRY

A once-a-week trip to the market or health-food store is all it will take to keep you well stocked. Planning ahead is the key to being able to whip together a meal, especially on short notice. The list of ingredients under the fridge, freezer, and pantry sections not only provides a basic shopping list for the menu plans that follow but also will assure you that you have a variety of healthy foods on hand when you are feeling creative and want to experiment on your own. Some brand names are given for your convenience.

Keep in mind that the variety of fresh fruits and vegetables changes by the season. I urge you to buy fresh produce when it is in season (and therefore at its peak nutritional and phyto-chemical value) and then add as much as you can to your meals. For all food groups, try to buy "certified organic" and look for the words "unrefined, low-heat, expeller-pressed" on labels of natural oils.

Stocking the Fridge

Oils Barlean's Flax Seed Oil, Barlean's Essential Woman Oil, sesame oil, canola oil, peanut oil

Dairy products Sweet butter, cheeses (low-fat ricotta cheese, low-fat cottage cheese, part-skim mozzarella [string cheese], feta, cheddar, Parmesan, Swiss), yogurt (nonfat plain, vanilla, maple, lemon), low-fat sour cream

Protein foods Organic eggs (omega-3 enriched eggs if possi-ble), tofu, tempeh

Nuts and seeds Almonds, cashews, pine nuts, hazelnuts, wal-nuts, pecans, pumpkin seeds, sunflower seeds, flaxseeds, sesame seeds, nut or seed butters (peanut, almond, tahini)

Fruits Lemons, limes, grapefruit, oranges, apples, kiwi, avocados

Vegetables Cabbage, celery, cucumbers, daikon,* romaine lettuce, mushrooms, kale, collards, mixed sprouts, broccoli, spinach, zucchini, asparagus, cauliflower

Juices Unsweetened orange juice, grapefruit juice, low-sodium V-8

Condiments Canola mayonnaise, Dijon mustard, tamari, Tabasco, sweet pickle relish, fresh garlic, fresh ginger, unsweetened apple butter, all-fruit jams, Westbrae Natural Fruit Sweetened Catsup

Stocking the Freezer

Protein foods Shelton's Turkey Hot Dogs, Shelton's Chicken Pot Pie, beef flank steak, chicken breasts, ground turkey, fish fillets, shelled and deveined shrimp, ground chuck, lamb chops

Vegetables Asparagus, chopped spinach, corn, peas, broccoli, okra

Fruits Unsweetened blueberries, raspberries, strawberries

Breads Whole-grain pita pockets, whole-grain English muffins, whole-grain waffles, Ezekiel 4:9 whole-grain sprouted bread, rye bread, corn tortillas

---

*A type of radish used in Japanese cuisine that is thought to help metabolize fat.

Stocking the Pantry

Oils Extra-virgin olive oil

Grains Brown rice, steel-cut oats, whole-grain pasta, blue corn chips, Wasa crackers

Canned fish Tuna (Progresso Light Tuna in Olive Oil, Chicken of the Sea Solid White Tuna in Spring Water), salmon, mackerel, sardines (packed in olive oil, mustard, or tomato sauce)

Canned goods Progresso Lentil Soup, beans (chickpeas, black beans, kidney beans), unsweetened pineapple chunks, cherries, tomato sauce, black pitted olives, bamboo shoots, water chestnuts

Dried items Unsulphured dried fruit (figs, dates, apricots, cranberries, raisins, currants)

Condiments Nonirradiated dried herbs and spices (dill, tarragon, parsley, cumin, celery seeds, curry, garlic, onion powder), salsa, vinegars (apple cider, balsamic, red wine, raspberry), marinated artichoke hearts, roasted red peppers, toasted wheat germ, bacon bits

Baking needs Aluminum-free baking powder (Rumford, Royal, or Featherweight brands); kudzu (a healthy cornstarch substitute), date sugar, blackstrap molasses, carob chips, nonalcohol vanilla, anise, almond, and lemon extracts

Miscellaneous Protein powders (Solgar's Whey to Go, Naturade's Fat-Free Vegetable Protein), Pacific Foods almond milk, rice milk

SAVVY SUBSTITUTES

So the toasted wheat germ has to go? And you really can't stand kale? These savvy substitutes will enable you to individualize the following menu plans to suit your own taste preferences. The only caveat here is to exchange one food for another from the same food category in the portions that are listed.

Essential and Healthy Fats: The Satiety Factor Nutrient

Oils

1 tablespoon oil (olive, sesame, peanut, or flaxseed)

½ small avocado

15 small nuts (almonds, cashews, pecans, walnuts, pine nuts, hazelnuts, pistachios, macadamias, peanuts)

1½ teaspoons seeds (sesame, pumpkin, sunflower)

1 tablespoon nut butter (almond, peanut, tahini)

1 tablespoon canola mayonnaise

Protein Power

2 eggs

3 ounces cooked meat (veal, poultry, lamb)

6 ounces fish or shellfish

½ cup tofu or tempeh

Vegetables—The More the Merrier

2 cups leafy greens, raw (spinach, romaine lettuce, arugula, or other leafy green)

½ cup cooked vegetable (broccoli, beets, kale, collards, okra, carrots, zucchini)

1 cup raw vegetable (celery, cucumber, radishes, mushrooms, green or red peppers)

Fruits—Color Is the Key
1 apple, pear, nectarine, peach, plum, kiwi
1 cup cantaloupe, watermelon, or honeydew chunks
1 cup blueberries, raspberries, or strawberries
½ grapefruit
10 grapes
12 cherries
½–¾ cup (or 4–6 ounces) fruit juice

Breads, Grains, and Starches
1 slice whole-grain bread, 1 tortilla, or ½ whole-grain pita pocket
½ whole-grain English muffin, ½ slice pumpernickel, or ½ whole-grain bagel
½ cup brown rice, whole-grain pasta, or other grain
½ cup winter squash, peas, corn, potatoes, sweet potatoes, lentils, beans, or split peas
2 tablespoons toasted wheat germ

Dairy—If You Dare
1 cup nonfat plain yogurt
½ cup part-skim ricotta cheese or low-fat cottage cheese
1 ounce Swiss or cheddar, or 1½ ounces part-skim mozzarella

BREAKTHROUGH BREAKFASTS

Here are seven different breakfasts from which to choose. Remember that it is essential you eat something in the morning that contains fat, protein, and carbohydrate to jump-start your system. When you eat yogurt, ricotta cheese, or cottage cheese, mix in a tablespoon of flaxseed oil or the Essential Woman Oil (a blend of flaxseed oil and evening primrose oil available in health-food stores). This is not only a tasty way to incorporate flaxseed oil with its beneficial omega-3 healing properties into the diet but also has another benefit. According to researchers in Germany, the sulfur-bearing amino acids in the dairy products combined with the essential fatty acids of the flaxseed oil are a potent breast cancer fighter.

Day 1

Strawberry smoothie (blending ½ cup sliced strawberries with 8 ounces of almond milk and 1 scoop of unflavored protein powder)

1 slice toasted multigrain bread with 1 teaspoon of sweet butter

Note: If a smoothie works for you on a daily basis, then vary the fruit (try blueberries, raspberries, banana, pineapple, or peaches) as well as the milk (oat milk or diluted rice milk can be substituted for the almond milk).

Day 2

6 ounces orange juice

Cheezy muffin (sprinkle 1 or 2 ounces shredded, part-skim

mozzarella over ½ whole-grain English muffin; broil until the cheese melts, top with tomato).

Day 3

1 cup cantaloupe chunks

1 cup vanilla fat-free yogurt with 1 tablespoon Essential Woman Oil and 2 tablespoons toasted wheat germ

Day 4

½ grapefruit

2 poached eggs topped with 2 tablespoon salsa on 1 or 2 warmed corn tortillas

Day 5

1 small kiwi

½ cup low-fat ricotta cheese with 1 tablespoon flaxseed oil

½ pumpernickel bagel

Day 6

½ cup low-fat cottage cheese with 1 tablespoon flaxseed oil

½ cup pineapple chunks

1 slice rye toast

Day 7

1 cup low-sodium V-8 juice

2 hard-cooked eggs

1 slice whole-grain toast with 1 tablespoon unsweetened apple butter

LITE 'N' ALIVE LUNCHES

Day 1

Mixed green salad made with dark leafy greens, cucumber slices, tomatoes, shredded carrots, and olives, with apple cider vinegar

Open-faced egg salad sandwich on rye made with 2 hard-boiled eggs, 1 tablespoon canola mayonnaise, chopped celery and onions

1 teaspoon Dijon mustard, dash of celery seeds

Day 2

1 bowl lentil soup

Spinach salad made with chopped spinach, sliced mushrooms, roasted red peppers, and bacon bits

1 tablespoon olive oil and fresh lemon juice dressing

Day 3—Fast-Food Lunch

McDonald's Grilled Chicken Salad Deluxe

Lite vinaigrette dressing

Day 4

Greek salad made with 3 ounces feta cheese, tomatoes, Bermuda onion, lettuce, parsley, and marinated artichoke hearts

1 tablespoon olive oil and fresh lemon juice dressing

1 whole-grain pita pocket

Day 5

Tofu and vegetable stir fry made with 3 ounces tofu, water
   chestnuts, bok choy, baby corn, and bamboo shoots
   sautéed in 2 teaspoons peanut oil
½ cup brown rice or rice noodles

Day 6

Tuna fish salad made with 3 ounces tuna fish, 1 tablespoon
   canola mayonnaise, chopped celery, chopped leeks, and
   a dash of curry
Romaine lettuce and tomatoes with lemon

Day 7

Avocado salad made with ½ small avocado, onions, tomatoes,
   and ½ cup garbanzos
Mixed salad greens with toasted walnuts and balsamic vinegar

DELITEFUL DINNERS

Day 1

6 ounces broiled salmon prepared with 2 teaspoons olive oil
   and 1 tablespoon tamari
Medley of steamed zucchini, yellow squash, and snap peas
Grated daikon, carrot, and onion salad drizzled with apple
   cider vinegar

Day 2—Fast-Food Dinner

2 Taco Bell grilled chicken burritos (just a dollop of cheese or
      sour cream, please!) with mild taco sauce and pico
      de gallo
Lots of lettuce and tomato

Day 3

4 ounces turkey burger with sweet pickle relish
½ cup brown rice with 3 tablespoons toasted pecan pieces
Steamed asparagus
Cole slaw

Day 4

4 ounces broiled lamb chop brushed with 1 teaspoon Dijon
      mustard
½ cup baked acorn squash drizzled before serving with
      2 teaspoons flaxseed oil
1 cup steamed kale and button mushrooms

Day 5

Cucumber soup (combine 1 cup low-fat yogurt with 2 cups
      peeled, seeded, puréed cucumber and 1 teaspoon dill)
4 ounces shrimp with bean sprouts, red and green cabbage,
      and carrots stir-sautéed in 1 tablespoon peanut oil
½ cup peas

Day 6

4 ounces baked scrod with tarragon
½ cup steamed collards with 1 tablespoon sesame oil
1 small sweet potato
Chopped parsley, tomato, and scallions with lemon

Day 7

1 cup whole-grain pasta with 4 ounces turkey meatballs and
    marinara sauce
Radish and watercress salad with 1 tablespoon olive oil and
    balsamic vinegar

Bibliography

Adlercreutz, Mazur. "Phyto-estrogens and Western Diseases." *Annals of Medicine* 29 (1997): 95–120.

American Institute for Cancer Research Newsletter, "Feast on Phyto-chemicals." (Spring 1996): 1–12.

Atkins, Robert. *Dr. Atkins' Health Revelations.* Frederick, Md.: Agora Publishers, 1998.

———. *Dr. Atkins' Vita-Nutrient Solution.* New York: Simon & Schuster, 1998.

Ballentine, Rudolph, M.D. "Choosing a Cooking Medium: Butter vs. Oil." *East/West Journal* (February 1988): 38–43.

Barilla, Jean, ed. *The Nutrition Superbook 2: The Good Fats and Oils.* Los Angeles: Keats Publishing, 1996.

Beutler, Jade. "High in Lignan Flax Oil." *Health Perspectives* 3, no. 2 (1997): 1–2.

Brody, Jane. "Trans Fatty Acids Tied to Risk of Breast Cancer." *New York Times* (October 14, 1997).

———. "Women's Heart Risk Linked to Types of Fats, Not Total." *New York Times* (November 20, 1997): A1, A26.

Burros, Marian. "Losing Count of Calories as Plates Fill Up." *New York Times* (April 2, 1997).

Chin, S. F., et al. "Conjugated Linoleic Acid Is a Growth Factor for Rats as Shown by Enhanced Weight Gain and Improved Feed Efficiency." *Journal of Nutrition* 124, no. 12 (1994): 2344–49.

de Lorgeril, M., P. Salen, and J. Delaye. "Effect of a Mediterranean Type of Diet on the Rate of Cardiovascular Complications in Patients with Coronary Artery Disease." *Journal of the American College of Cardiology* 28, no. 5 (1996): 1103–8.

de Lorgeril, M., S. Renaud, and J. Delaye. "Mediterranean Alpha-Linoleic Acid-Rich Diet in Secondary Prevention of Coronary Heart Disease." *The Lancet* 343 (1994): 1454–545.

Dolecek, T. A., and G. Grandits. "Dietary Polyunsaturated Fatty Acids and Mortality in Multiple Risk Factor Intervention Trial." *World Review of Nutrition and Diet* 66 (1991): 205–16.

Dyerberg, J., and H. O. Bang. "Eicosapentaenoic Acid and Prevention of Thrombosis and Atherosclerosis." *Lancet* 2 (1978): 117.

———. "Lipid Metabolism, Atherogenesis and Haemostasis in Eskimos: The Role of the Prostaglandin-3 Family." *Haemostasis* 8 (1979): 227.

Eades, Michael, and Mary Dan Eades. *Protein Power: The Metabolic Breakthrough*. New York: Bantam Books, 1996.

Eaton S. B., and Melvin Konne. "Paleolithic Nutrition: A Consideration of its Nature and Current Implications." *New England Journal of Medicine* 312, no. 5 (1985): 283–89.

Eaton S. B., M. Shostak, and M. Konner. *The Paleolithic Prescription*. New York: Harper & Row, 1988.

Enig, Mary, Ph.D. "Trans Fatty Acids in the Food Supply: A Comprehensive Report Covering 60 Years of Research." Silver Spring, Md.: Enig Associates, 1993.

Fallon, Sally W., M.A., and Mary G. Enig, Ph.D. "Why Butter is Better." *Health Freedom News* (November/December 1995): 12–15.

Finnegan, John. "The Revolution in Oil Production." *Townsend Letter for Doctors* (February/March 1995): 68–69.

Fraser, G. E., et al. "A Possible Protective Effect of Nut Consumption on Risk of Coronary Heart Disease—The Adventist Health Study." *Archives of Internal Medicine* 152, no. 7 (1992): 1416–24.

Fuller, C. J. "Effects of Antioxidants and Fatty Acids on Low Density Lipoprotein Oxidation." *American Journal of Clinical Nutrition* 60, no. 6 (supplement) (December 1994): 1010F–13F.

Gapinski, J. P., et al. "Preventing Restinosis with Fish Oils Following Coronary Angioplasty." *Archives of Internal Medicine* 153 (1993): 1595–601.

Gittleman, Ann Louise, M.S., C.N.S. *Beyond Pritikin*. New York: Bantam Books, 1988.

———. "The Essential Woman: Super-Nutrients for Women Throughout Their Life Cycle." *Health Perspectives* 3, no. 6 (1997): 1–2.

———. *Get the Sugar Out: 501 Simple Ways to Cut the Sugar Out of Any Diet*. New York: Crown, 1996.

———. *The 40/30/30 Phenomenon*. Los Angeles: Keats Publishing, 1997.

Gladwell, Malcolm. "The Pima Paradox." *The New Yorker* (February 1998): 44–57.

Grady, Denise. "Study Favors Monounsaturated Fat." *New York Times* (January 13, 1998).

Grundy, Scott, M.D. "Comparison of Monounsaturated Fatty Acids and Carbohydrates for Lowering Plasma Cholesterol." *New England Journal of Medicine* 314, no. 12 (1986): 745.

———. "Multifactorial Causation of Obesity: Implications for Prevention." *American Journal of Clinical Nutrition* 67 (supplement) (March 1998): 563S–72S.

Hainault, I., M. Carlotti, and M. Lavau. "Fish Oil in a High Lard Diet Prevents Obesity, Hyperlipemia and Adipocyte Insulin Resistance in Rats." *Annals of New York Academy of Sciences*, 98–101.

Harris, William, Ph.D. "Fish Oils, Omega-3 Polyunsaturated Fatty Acids, and Coronary Heart Disease." *The PUFA Information Backgrounder* (July 1997).

Heller, Richard, and Rachael Heller. *The Carbohydrate Addict's Diet*. New York: NAL Dutton, 1992.

Holman, R. T. "Significance of Essential Fatty Acids in Human Nutrition" *Lipids* 1 (1976): 215.

Horrobin, David F., M.D., Ph.D. *Clinical Uses of Essential Fatty Acids.* Montreal, London: Eden Press, 1982.

————. "The Regulation of Prostaglandin Biosynthesis by the Manipulation of Essential Fatty Acid Metabolism." Rev. *Drug Metabolism Drug Interaction* 4 (1983): 339.

————. "The Prostaglandins' Physiology, Pharmacology and Clinical Aspects." St. Albans, Vt.: Eden Medical Research, 1978.

————. "Nutritional and Medical Importance of Gamma-Linoleic Acid." *Progress in Lipid Research* 31 (1992): 163–94.

Hu, Frank, M.D. "Dietary Fat Intake and the Risk of Coronary Heart Disease in Women." *New England Journal of Medicine* 337, no. 21 (November 20, 1997): 1491–99.

Jialial, I. "Influence of Antioxidant Vitamins on LDL Oxidation." *Annals of the New York Academy of Sciences* (September 30, 1992): 237–47.

Kolata G. "Cholesterol's New Image: High Is Bad; So Is Low." *New York Times* (August 11, 1992).

Kurzer, M. S., L. Slavin, and H. Adlercreutz. "Flaxseed, Lignans, and Sex Hormones." *Flaxseed in Human Nutrition*, S. C. Cunane, and L. U. Thompson, eds. Champaign, Ill.: AOCS Press, 1995.

Levenstein, Barbara, M.S. "How to Tell a 'Good' Fat from a 'Bad' One." *The EFA Quarterly Report* 1, no. 4.

Levine, Barbara, Ph.D. "Why You Need DHA." *Let's Live* (February 1998): 124.

Lombard, Jay, and Carl Germano. *The Brain Wellness Plan.* New York: Kensington, 1998.

McCully, Kilmer S., M.D. *The Homocysteine Revolution.* Los Angeles: Keats Publishing, 1997.

Maffetone, Phillip. "The New Dietary Ethic: Eat Fat to Lose Weight and Go Faster." *Bicycling* (January 1995): 52–53.

Mason, Michael. "Welcome Fat Back Into Your Kitchen." *Health* (April 1997): 69–73.

Mason, Michelle. "Confessions of a Fat-Free Snack Junkie." *Health* (May/June 1995): 36, 42.

Morris, M. C., et al. "Fish Consumption and Cardiovascular Disease in the Physicians' Health Study." *American Journal of Epidemiology* 142 (1995): 166–75.

Mowrey, Daniel B., Ph.D. *Fat Management! The Thermogenic Factor.* Lehi, Utah: Victory Publications, 1994.

Mudd, Chris. *Cholesterol and Your Health.* Oklahoma City, Okla.: American Lite Company, 1988.

Murray, Michael T., N.D., and Jade Beutler. *Understanding Fats and Oils.* Encinitas, Calif.: Progressive Health Publishing, 1996.

Nunziato, Dina. "Super Immune Boosters." *Healthy Mind/Healthy Body* (Fall 1997).

O'Neill, Molly, "So It May Be True After All: Eating Pasta Makes You Fat." *New York Times* (February 8, 1995): A1, C6.

Ornish, Dean, M.D. *Eat More, Weigh Less.* New York: HarperCollins, 1993.

Oster, P., et al. *Research in Experimental Medicine.* (Berlin) 175: 287–91.

Pariza, M., et. al. "Conjugated Linoleic Acid (GLA) Reduces Body Fat." *Experimental Biology Conference,* Abstract, 1996

———. "Conjugated Linoleic Acid (GLA) Reduces Body Fat." *FASEB Journal* 10, no. 3 (1996): A560.

Plotnick, Gary, M.D. "Effect of Antioxidant Vitamins on the Impairment of Endothelium Dependent Brachial Artery Vasoactivity Following a Single High Fat Meal." *Journal of the American Medical Association* 278 (November 26, 1997): 1682–2168.

Renaud, S., and T. Paul. "Cretan Mediterranean Diet for Prevention of Coronary Heart Disease." *American Journal of Clinical Nutrition* 61 (supplement) (1995): 1360S–7S.

Rudin, Donald, M.D. "The Dominant Diseases of Modernized Societies as Omega-3 Essential Fatty Acid Deficiency Syndrome: Substrate Beriberi." *Medical Hypotheses* 8:17, 1982.

———. "The Major Psychoses and Neuroses as Omega-3 Essential Fatty Acid Deficiency Syndrome: Substrate Pellagra." *Biological Psychiatry* 16:837, 1981.

Rudin, Donald, M.D., and Clara Felix. *Omega-3 Oils*. Garden City Park, N.Y.: Avery, 1996.

Salmeron, Jorge, et al. "Dietary Fiber, Glycemic Load, and the Risk of Non-Insulin-Dependent Diabetes Mellitus in Women." *JAMA* 277, no. 6 (February 12, 1997): 472–77.

Salmon, M. B. "Breast Milk: Nature's Perfect Formula." Techkits, Inc., P.O. Box 105, Demarest, N.J., 1994.

Sanders, T. A. B., et al. "Influence of Omega-3 Fatty Acids on Blood Lipids in Normal Subjects." *Journal of International Medicine* 225 (Supplement 1) 1989: 99–104.

Simon, J. A., et al. "Serum Fatty Acids and the Risk of Stroke." *Stroke* 26 (1995): 778–82.

Simopoulos, Artemis P., M.D. "Omega-3 Fatty Acids in Health and Disease and in Growth and Development." *The American Journal of Clinical Nutrition* 54 (1991): 438–63.

Simopoulos, Artemis P., M.D., and Jo Robinson. *The Omega Plan*. New York: HarperCollins, 1998.

Vaddadi, K. S., and D. F. Horrobin. "Weight Loss Produced by Evening Primrose Oil Administration in Normal and Schizophrenic Individuals." *IRCS Medical Science* (1979): 52.

Willet, W. C. "Diet and Health: What Should We Eat?" *Science* 264 (1994): 532–37.

Willet, W. C., et al. "Intake of Trans-fatty Acids and Risk of Coronary Heart Disease Among Women." *Lancet* 341 (1993): 581–85.

Zerden, Sheldon. *The Cholesterol Hoax: 101 + Lies*. Carson City, Nev.:
    Bridger House Publishers, 1997.
Zimmerman, Marcia, M.Ed., C.N. "Avoiding Fat Free Rebound: Part I."
    Nature's Impact (October/November 1997): 45–47.
———. "Avoiding Fat Free Rebound: Part II." *Nature's Impact*
    (December 1997/January 1998): 32–35.

Index

UniKey Health Systems
Bozeman, Montana 59771
(800) 888-4353
unikey@unikeyhealth.com
www.unikeyhealth.com

This company is a source for all my books including *Beyond Pritikin* and *Get the Sugar Out*. UniKey also distributes many dietary supplements such as MaxEPA, GLA, flaxseed oil capsules, and Barlean's Essential Woman Oil. Ask for the latest catalogue.